Understanding Second Language Learning and Teaching

Understanding Second Language Learning and Teaching

Printed in 2024. 6. 14.
Published in 2024. 6. 24.

Author Kim Ji Hyun
Publisher Synn Ilhi
Published by Keimyung University Press
Room 105 Bosangwan, Keimyung University
1095 Dalgubeoldaero, Dalseo Gu, Daegu 42601
TEL. +82-53-580-6233 FAX. +82-53-580-6235
Homepage. www.kmupress.com
Registration 1970. 9. 1. (#347-1998-1)

ISBN 979-11-6516-230-6 93740 Price ₩ 20,000

Understanding Second Language Learning and Teaching

Ji Hyun Kim

KEIMYUNG UNIVERSITY PRESS

Preface

"Understanding Second Language Learning and Teaching" aims to introduce key learning theories and relevant teaching approaches. A solid grasp of language learning theories is crucial for educators to effectively design and deliver lessons. However, given the complicated nature of language acquisition, comprehending these theories can be challenging. Hence, I have strived to clarify these concepts in a more accessible manner. Each chapter incorporates 'Things to Consider' sections, prompting readers to reflect on their own teaching and learning experiences, and these sections can also facilitate the application of learning theories to practical contexts. Furthermore, theories are explained through abundant examples where feasible, aiding readers in comprehending the complexities of the learning process. Additionally, teaching approaches are presented alongside theories to help readers grasp the connection between learning and teaching more clearly.

This book comprises 8 chapters and each chapter explores various aspects of second language acquisition. Chapter 1 explains the definition of second language acquisition and crucial concepts for comprehending the learning process. Chapter 2 covers behaviorism, an early language learning theory, along with its corresponding teaching approaches. In Chapter 3, another significant early theory, UG theory, is introduced. It also discusses Krashen's Model and relevant teaching approaches. Chapter 4 explores the cognitive approach, laying the groundwork for contemporary instructed second language acquisition theories. It encompasses major cognitive theories and relevant practices in second language learning. Chapter 5 addresses the evolution in second language teaching methodologies. Chapter 6 deals with the instruction approach, focusing on form, recognized as a balanced instructional method for second language acquisition. Chapter 7 includes sociocultural theory and its integration into second language classrooms. Finally, Chapter 8 deals with learner individual differences, explaining how these differences impact learning outcomes across diverse learners.

It is my hope that this book provides language teachers including pre-service teachers with fundamental knowledge and valuable insights into language learning and teaching, serving as a roadmap in their pursuit of becoming proficient second language educators. Furthermore, it can serve as a valuable resource for university instructors teaching courses on second language learning and teaching.

Contents

Chapter 1

Introduction

1. What is Second Language Acquisition (SLA)?

2. Learning Contexts

3. Three Key Terms You Should Know

Chapter 1

Introduction

Whar is Second Languga Acquisition (SLA)?

Second language acquisition (SLA) is the academic field that investigates how people learn languages other than first language (L1) once they have acquired L1. Thus, the term of second language (L2) encompasses all languages (including a second language, a third language, etc.) learned beyond the acquisition of one's L1 (Ortega, 2009).

We can easily imagine how complex the process of SLA might be. It seems impossible to explain the process whereby human beings acquire the L2 using a particular theoretical framework. Accordingly, SLA has been developed as multi- and inter-disciplinary field which includes a variety of academic areas such as linguistics, child L1 studies, sociolinguistics, psychology, sociology, neuro-linguistics, education, and so on. SLA inquires a swathe of complex factors and phenomena that contribute to learning outcomes in a wide range of contexts.

Learning Contexts

Then, what does mean by learning contexts? Simply put, think about the environments learners are exposed to and/or experience while they learn the second language (L2). There are many different ways to differentiate learning environments. One typical way is to divide the contexts into naturalistic and instructed settings. Naturalistic learners learn the L2 through informal opportunities in multicultural neighborhoods and workplaces, without receiving any organized instruction. In contrast, instructed learners learn the L2 through formal study in schools, private institutes, and so on. As a matter of fact, in our globalized world, it might not be feasible to define the learning contexts using this dichotomy approach. L2 learners are exposed to diverse opportunities for L2 learning through travel, migration, occupation, marriage, and so on. Therefore, it can be said that most of the people acquire additional languages from a mixture of both naturalistic and instructed experiences.

Learning contexts can also be classified into second language contexts and foreign language contexts. You may be familiar with the words ESL and/or EFL. These are the abbreviations for English as a second/foreign language. Then, we need to know the difference between second and foreign languages. Consider the following two cases:

Case 1: You study English in your native country. (of course, your mother togue is not English.)
Case 2: You study English in England.

In Case 1, you are referred to as an EFL learner, whereas in Case 2, you are labeled as an ESL learner. The distinction lies in the fact that in Case 1, English is not the official or national language of the region, while in Case 2, English is the national language of England. It is clear that there is a difference between second language and foreign language acquisition. In the majority of cases, English is considered a foreign language, and individuals are learning it within the context of EFL.

Although the terms, second and foreign languages, have a different interpretation, you can easily see many cases where these two are interchangeably used without any distinction. However, it is important to acknowledge the difference and to use them properly when you specifically discuss the differences of learning contexts.

Things to Consider 1.1

1. Have you learned other languages rather than your native language? If so, how can you classify your learning contexts of the language(s)?

2. Compare the naturalistic and instructed settings.

	Strengths	Weaknesses
Naturalistic setting		
Instructed setting		

3. Compare the ESL and EFL settings.

	ESL	EFL
Exposures		
Production		
Instruction		
Strengths		
Weaknesses		

Three Key Terms You Should Know

There are numerous terms you should understand and remember in order to understand the process of SLA. Here, as a start, you will be introduced three key terms. Read the passage below, and guess the meanings of the terms **in bold**.

When we learn a language, regardless of L1 and L2, exposure to language **input** is essential. Although learning theories have differently valued the amount and quality of **input** necessary for language learning, all admit that no one learns a language without **input**. Of course, all **input** learners have received do not turn into **intake**. Learners would not process and/or understand some of the **input**, but they would some of them. **Input** which has been processed could be a source of L2 learning. In addition, learners' understanding **input** does not guarantee that they can make **output** of it. Consider the case where you understand what your interlocutor is saying to you in L2 but you do not know how to answer or respond to her. Yes, you need **input** for **output**, but it takes time for you to process **input** and develop a system that eventually leads you to make L2 **output**.

Things to Consider 1.2

Now consider the questions below:

1. Can you make a diagram which explains the relationship between input and intake?
2. Can you make a diagram which explains the process of L2 using the terms input, intake, and output?

Chapter Summary

This chapter has introduced the concept of second language acquisition (SLA) and highlighted important terms crucial for understanding the SLA process. While SLA is intricate, individuals interested in teaching and learning a second language (L2) must have a solid understanding of it to facilitate effective L2 instruction. Simply put, effective L2 teaching is not possible without a comprehensive understanding of how learners acquire the language. As you continue to study the following chapters of this book, you will gain the necessary insights into SLA, enabling you to apply this understanding to the specific teaching context you find yourself in.

Chapter 2

Early Theory of SLA and Teaching Approach 1

Chapter 2

Early Theory of SLA and Teaching Approach 1

Have you ever heard about Pavlov's Dog Experiment? If you have or have not, you can easily find what it is through the Internet. Shall we?

Things to Consider 2.1

1. What are the words you have found important in this experiment?
2. Can you guess how Pavlov accounted for 'learning' using this experiment?

Numerous theories and principles have been proposed to explain second language learning processes.

In this chapter, you will study one of the early theories that continues to shape second language teaching - Behaviorism. This theory is linked with Pavlov's experiment and provides a framework for understanding the process of learning a second language.

Behaviorism

Behaviorism is a psychological theory concerning the behavior of animals and humans. It states that all behaviors are learned through conditioned interaction with the environment, emphasizing that behaviors are shaped by environmental stimuli (Pavlov, 1932; Skinner, 1965).

In Pavlov's experiment, a sound was played every time the dogs were given food. Thus, when the dogs heard the sound (the stimulus), they anticipated a meal, and they would begin salivating (the response). What this experiment demonstrated was that even when the sound was played without food being presented, the dogs would still salivate due to the repeated association between the sound and feeding. Behaviorists apply similar principles to human behavior. For instance, they argue that a child will form a habit of crying to get attention from a caregiver (parent) if crying consistently leads to being picked up. If the crying does not bring about the desired attention, the child will eventually abandon this strategy. This emphasis on learning through the formation of associations is the fundamental characteristic of behaviorism.

Behaviorists argued that this process did not involve cognitive activities; it was entirely a result of the association of events, reacting to environmental stimuli and followed by reinforcement or punishment. Essentially, both of these are responses to the response. Reinforcement motivates the continuation of the response behavior, while punishment acts to discourage the repetition of the response.

Things to Consider 2.2

Let's apply this logic to Tom's case:

Tom, a two-years old boy, needed assistance to get a toy from the shelf at Toys "R" Us. As he glanced around, he overheard someone requesting, "Could you get a blue one, please?" She got what she wanted. Inspired by this, Tom also pointed at a toy, repeating the word "please, please." A nearby clock fetched the toy for him. Next day, Tom said to his mom, "Milk, please". He got his milk.

1. What would Tom say whenever he wants something?
2. Can you explain Tom's behavior using the concepts of 'stimulus-response and reinforcement'?
3. Do you think Tom would have said 'please' to his mom if he hadn't been able to get the toy?

Within the behaviorist theory, all learning, including language, involves forming habits through the establishment of stimulus-response associations that are reinforced over time, thereby becoming stronger.

Behaviorism and Language Learning

From this point of view, the environment in which language learners find themselves plays an essential role since consistent stimuli, responses, and either positive or negative reinforcement (like praise/successful dialogue or communication breakdown) is necessary for learning. During the acquisition of their first language, children imitate the sounds and patterns they hear in their surroundings (a process known as stimulus-response). When children attempt to reproduce the language they have heard, if their efforts are typically met with positive reinforcement such as praise or successful interaction, this can motivate them to continue mimicking and practicing these sounds and patterns until they become habits of accurate language use.

Learning a first language is comparatively simple: it primarily involves learning a set of habits by mimicking and repeating them as noted above. However, when it comes to learning a second language, we encounter challenges due to deeply established habits from our native language. Thus, the process of learning a new language necessitates the displacement of these existing habits with a fresh set of habits.

The obstacle is that the old L1 habits interfere this process, either helping or preventing. If the structures in the second language (L2) align with those in L1, then learning becomes a smoother process. However, if the structures are different, then learning process can be more challenging. As Lado put it:

> We know from the observation of many cases that the grammatical structure of the native language tends to be transferred to the foreign language... we have here the major source of difficulty or ease in learning the foreign language... Those structures that are different will be difficult. (Lado,

1957, pp. 58-59, cited in Dulay et al., 1982, p. 99)

Things to Consider 2.3

1. Have you had any personal learning experiences that verify Lado's assertion?
2. Have you had any personal learning experiences that do not support Lado's claim?

Contrastive Analysis

To determine the similarity between the structures of a first language (L1) and a second language (L2), the initial step involves contrasting L1 structures with those of L2. Researchers took on the huge task of comparing between pairs of languages, a process known as Contrastive Analysis.

The contrastive analysis hypothesis suggests that positive transfer takes place when languages share similarities, allowing learners to use their established habits from their first language with little difficulty. On the other hand, when languages differ, negative transfer takes place, which can lead to challenges and errors for learners. Such errors are referred to as *interference errors* or *transfer errors*. The foundational assumptions of the contrastive analysis hypothesis can be summarized as follows:

1. Contrastive analysis is based on a theory of language that

claims that language is habit and that language learning involves the establishment of a new set of habits.

2. The major source of error in the production and/or reception of a second language is the native language.
3. One can account for errors by considering differences between the first language and the second language.
4. A corollary to item 3 is that the greater the differences, the more errors will occur.
5. What one has to do in learning a second language is learn the differences. Similarities can be safely ignored as no new learning is involved. In other words, what is dissimilar between two languages is what must be learned.
6. Difficulty and ease in learning is determined receptively by differences and similarities between the two languages in contrast.

(Adapted from Gass & Selinker, 2008, pp. 96-97)

Identifying the similarities and discrepancies between languages enables predictions about which areas will be effortless or challenging for learners. This is the ultimate goal of contrastive analysis. Additionally, it allows for the identification of potential errors, and decisions can be made about what needs to be learned and what is unnecessary in the context of second language learning.

Things to Consider 2.4

Given what we have covered so far regarding Behaviorism and the Contrastive Analysis Hypothesis (CAH), what actions should teachers of a second language (L2) be taking in the classroom?

Behaviorism, Contrastive Analysis, and Language Teaching

From an instructional perspective, behaviorism and the Contrastive Analysis Hypothesis (CAH) have two main implications. First, teachers need to concentrate their teaching efforts on structures which are believed to be difficult, and as mentioned previously, difficult structures would be those that differ between the learner's first language (L1) and the second language (L2) they are trying to learn. Second, optimal learning conditions are achieved when there is an abundance of precise models and feedback is given instantly and consistently. Learners should be exposed to a large number of target examples of language; they should imitate these examples repeatedly and receive suitable feedback - positive reinforcement for accurate imitation, and correction for inaccurate ones. This cycle should be repeated until the behaviors become a habit. This approach has had an impact on second language teaching strategies, with the audiolingual method serving as a prime example.

Audiolingual Method

The audiolingual method initiated from the Army Specialized Program established in 1942 to train the US military in foreign languages as the country entered World War II. Linguists were hired to aid in language teaching and material development. Charles Fries, a scholar of structural linguistics, was the key figure in developing this method in 1945, integrating elements of structural linguistics and behavioral psychology.

This approach considered the grammar of a language as the fundamental starting point for learning. It claimed that the unique sound units of a language form its structure, which further create lexical and grammatical elements, eventually constituting higher structures like phrases and sentences.

Under the audiolingual method, teaching focuses heavily on the practice of fundamental sentence patterns through rigorous oral drills. The primary goal is to improve oral skills, and hence, lessons are predominantly dialogue-based, carried out in the language being taught. It puts a strong emphasis on memorizing through repetition and achieving correct pronunciation from the very start. The method also highlights an inductive approach to teaching grammar, presented in a planned and sequenced manner.

Learners are primarily expected to orally reproduce memorized dialogues, and any errors are promptly corrected to prevent them from becoming habits. As the teacher only needs proficiency in the structures and learning materials, fluency in the language being taught is not a requisite. This method is particularly effective in large class settings.

Here are some examples of dialogues that could be used to teach 'be going to' using the audiolingual method. The idea is to present the dialogues and then have the students practice them repetitively until they can use the form correctly and fluently. Note that these dialogues focus only on the use of 'be going to' to discuss future plans or intentions.

Dialogue 1

Sue: Hello, John. What are you going to do tomorrow?

John: Hello, Sue. I am going to visit the museum tomorrow.

Sue: That sounds interesting. Who is going with you?

John: My friend, Lisa, is going to go with me.

Dialogue 2

Peter: Good morning, Lisa. Are you going to watch the football match this weekend?

Lisa: Good morning, Peter. Yes, I am going to watch the football match.

Peter: Great! Who is going to win?

Lisa: I think our school team is going to win.

After practicing these dialogues several times, the teacher can then move on to controlled practice activities where students can substitute different vocabulary while maintaining the same grammar structure. It is essential to correct any errors immediately to prevent them from becoming a habit.

Things to Consider 2.5

1. Have you ever experienced learning a foreign or second

language using the audiolingual approach? If yes, could you share your experiences?

2. Can you explain the concept of the inductive method in language instruction? How does it contrast with the deductive method?
3. How does the audiolingual approach align with the principles of the inductive method?

Things to Consider 2.6

1. Which aspects of the theories and interpretations of behaviorism, CAH, and the audiolingual method do you find plausible or logical?
2. Which aspects of the theories and interpretations of behaviorism, CAH, and the audiolingual method do you find confusing or unconvincing?

Behaviorism Facing Criticisms

Starting in the 1950s and continuing in the 1970s, there were significant advancements in the fields of psychology and linguistics, which led to critiques of behavioral approaches to learning. The field of linguistics transitioned from a focus on structural linguistics, which was based on the description of the surface structures of a large corpus of language, to generative linguistics, which stressed the rule-governed and creative nature of human language. This shift was initiated by research into first language acquisition and the works of Noam Chomsky. In particular, Chomsky's detailed critique of Skinner's 'Verbal Behavior' in 1957, which outlined in detail behaviorists' views on language learning, had substantial effects. Chomsky's criticisms focused on two key issues:

1. The creativity of language: children do not just learn and repeat a large set of sentences, but they routinely create new sentences they have never previously heard. This is only possible because they internalize rules, not just sequences of words. (e.g., Mom goed, sheeps, etc.)
2. Considering the complexity and abstractness of linguistic rules, it is astonishing that children are able to master them so quickly and efficiently, especially given the scarce input they are provided with. Additionally, children are usually corrected based on the accuracy of what they say, not its structure. Even when the form of their speech is corrected, it does not appear to significantly impact the development of language structure.

Based on these observations, Chomsky argued that children possess an innate faculty which supports them in their learning of language. Children are innately wired to recognize the rules within a set of speech, and this process is guided by an innate knowledge of how these rules are structured. Discussion of Chomsky's theories will be continued and explored further in Chapter 3.

Evidence contradicting the theories of behaviorists and the Contrastive Analysis Hypothesis (CAH) has also been found in L2 studies. The contrastive analysis hypothesis assumes that the first language shapes the learning of a second language, allowing the prediction of learner errors by analyzing the differences between the two languages. However, a considerable number of studies (Dušková, 1984; Kellerman, 1987; Zobl, 1980) have found evidence that challenges this theory, demonstrating that errors in learning a second language cannot be solely attributed to the influence of the learner's first language.

For example, Zobl (1980), which studied both French speakers learning English and English speakers learning French, discovered inconsistencies in the actual errors made by the learners. In French, object pronoun precedes the verb, and in English, object pronouns follow the verb as in the example below:

> Je les vois. (I them see)
> I see them.

Based on the contrastive analysis hypothesis, we can easily predict that French speakers would make sentences like **I them see*, following French word order while English speakers would produce a sentence like **Je vois les*, using the English word order. However, the following data emerged in learner data:

> **By French learners of English**
> I see them. (produced)
> *I them see. (not produced)

> **By English learners of French**

*Je vois elle.

(I see her.)

*Le chien a mange les.

(The dog has eaten them.)

French learners of English never used the object pronoun according to French word order; instead, they correctly adhered to English structure, even though it contradicts French word order. In contrast, English learners of French followed the word order of their native language. This inconsistency raises the question: if the first language is the driving force, why is its influence not consistent between the two groups? In this case, contrastive analysis can describe the errors made by English learners, but it fails to explain why French learners correctly used English order in their production.

In addition, the errors made by second language learners are not always caused by the interference from their first language. L2 learners often commit errors that are also found in children's development of their first language. For instance, L2 learners of English make an error such as "*He goed there yesterday," applying regular rules to an irregular verb, a phenomenon known as overgeneralization. Interestingly, native English-speaking children often make the same error. Thus, this type of error is not exclusively linked to the influence of a second language learner's first language. Instead, it is classified as *developmental errors*. All learners, whether they are learning English as a first or second language, commonly make this type of errors as they grasp the concept of past tense in English.

One might also assume that second language learners with various native languages would commit different errors, as these errors would be caused by the interference of their first language. However, analyses on learner errors studies reveal that many errors, such as omitting specific grammatical elements (e.g., 3rd person -s, past tense *-ed*, etc.) or spelling inaccuracies, are consistently made by English learners, regardless of their first language backgrounds.

The behaviorists' perspective on language learning, along with the contrastive analysis hypothesis, were called into question by a great deal of empirical evidence. This evidence indicated that L2 learning could not be solely explained through the formation of new habits and L1 interference.

Chapter Summary

Behaviorism, an early psychological theory, seeks to explain human psychology, behaviors, and the process of learning. Despite facing criticism and disproof, particularly in the context of language acquisition, there is some partial agreement with its perspectives, particularly regarding the early stages of language learning (especially in L2) and the impact of learners' native language (L1) on their L2 learning process. In other words, while acknowledging the limitations of this theory in explaining the complete language learning process, it still contributes a valuable perspective to understanding certain aspects of it. Furthermore, although the Audiolingual method, aligned with this principle, is criticized for its limitations in fostering fluency in second language (L2) learners, it continues to be employed in numerous L2 classrooms, primarily due to its practicality rather than its proven effectiveness. Nevertheless, it is essential to recognize that some of its techniques are still believed useful, particularly for beginners.

As mentioned earlier, there is a necessity for additional explanations beyond the perspectives offered by behaviorism. In the upcoming chapters, we will explore and discuss core theories of second language (L2) learning, which will provide insights to address numerous unanswered questions left by behaviorism.

Chapter 3

Early Theory of SLA and Teaching Approach 2

1. Universal Grammar

2. Krashen's Monitor Model

3. Natural Approach

4. Chapter Summary

Chapter 3

Early Theory of SLA and Teaching Approach 2

Things to Consider 3.1

In Chapter 2, we had a sneak peek of Chomsky's perspectives on child language learning: Chomsky argued that children possess an innate faculty which supports them in their learning of language. Children are innately wired to recognize the rules within a set of speech, and this process is guided by an innate knowledge of how these rules are structured.

1. Do you think that human beings are born with the ability to acquire their L1?
2. Can you describe the process by which children acquire their first language?
3. Do you think you can explain the process of learning a second language (L2) using the same way you used in order to explain the first language learning? Why or why not?

Universal Grammar

In the early 1960s, research into how children acquire their first language disclosed that their speech patterns were not merely based on imitation. Instead, it was observed that children have an innate ability for language learning. Chomsky (1959), one of the most influential linguists, is at the center of this position. He posited that children are born with the equipment which specifically works for language learning, and this is termed the *language acquisition device* (LAD). The LAD is metaphorically referred to as a 'black box' holding universal principles common to all human languages. For this device to function, children just need exposure to language samples. These common principles across all human languages are known as Universal Grammar.

Within this model, both language production and comprehension stem from an abstract linguistic system, which is a mental representation of grammar that includes aspects like syntax, morphology, phonology, and semantics. Most of this knowledge is innate and does not necessarily have to be acquired when learning a first language. Instead, it emerges from Universal Grammar (UG). UG theory postulates that language is grounded in a collection of abstract principles that characterizes core grammars of all natural human languages. In addition to these principles that are invariable, there are parameters that vary across languages.

Cook (1997) provided an interesting explanation of these principles and parameters by comparing them to driving a car:

Overall, there is a principle that drivers have to keep consistently to one side of the road, which is taken for granted by all drivers in all countries. Exceptions to this principle, such as people driving down motorways on the wrong side, rate stories in the media or car chases in action movies. This principle does not, however, say, which side of the road people should drive on. A parameter of driving allows the side to be the left in England and Japan, and the right in the USA and France. Once a country has opted for one side or the other, it sticks to its choice: a change of setting is a massively complex operation… for the individual travelling from England to France. So, a universal principle and a variable parameter together sum up the essence of driving. The principle states the universal requirements on driving; the parameter specifies the variation between countries.

(Cook, 1997, pp. 250-251)

UG in First Language Acquisition

Universal Grammar (UG) is regarded as an innate language faculty that sets the boundaries for possible languages. This concept finds support in the observation that children can grasp complex grammatical rules without direct instruction. They acquire certain grammar properties that are not learnable from the language input they receive. Essentially, there is a disparity between the input children receive and what they ultimately learn, known as *the logical problem of language acquisition* or *the poverty of the stimulus*. White's 1989 study provides evidence for this notion through specific instances. Here are some examples to consider:

1. I want to go.
2. I wanna go.
3. John wants to go but we don't want to.
4. John wants to go but we don't wanna.
5. Do you want to look at the chickens?
6. Do you wanna look at the chickens?
7. Who do you want to see?
8. Who do you wanna see?

Examples 1-8 show the cases where 'want to' is replaced by 'wanna.' However, there are many instances where 'want to' cannot be replaced by 'wanna,' as in examples 9-12:

9. Who do you want to feed the dog?
10. *Who do you wanna feed the dog?
11. Who do you want to win the race?
12. *Who do you wanna win the race?

White (1989) claimed that children can discern when to use 'wanna' and when not to, even without explicit instruction on the grammatical rule highlighted by the examples above. However, determining the correct usage of 'want to' versus 'wanna' in informal English based solely on the input children receive is extremely challenging. White proposed that Universal Grammar (UG) assists children in grasping the rules governing the distribution of these English forms. Put simply, Sentence 7 can be represented as something like "You want to see X," while Sentence 9 can be represented as something like "You want X to feed the dog." In Sentence 7, 'want' and 'to' are contiguous, allowing contraction, whereas in Sentence 9, they are not. UG guides children to avoid constructing sentences like 10 and 12.

Furthermore, children naturally acquire the foundational structure and patterns of the language they are exposed to, regardless of the circumstances. Even in instances where they encounter incorrect grammar in their environment, they tend to learn the correct structures over time. This serves as evidence supporting the hypothesis that human beings possess an innate mechanism specifically dedicated to language acquisition.

UG in Second Language Acquisition

Although Chomsky did not explicitly outline the connection between Universal Grammar (UG) and second language acquisition, other linguists propose that UG provides the most appropriate framework for comprehending this process. They contend that UG continues to play a significant role during second language acquisition, serving as the primary driving force behind the process.

According to UG theory, effective second language acquisition involves learners adjusting certain language-specific settings, referred to as *parameter resetting*. For instance, one universal principle of language is the presence of a grammatical subject. However, the necessity of using a subject in declarative sentences varies across languages, constituting a parameter. In English, one can say "He speaks," but it is impossible to say "Speaks": declarative sentences must include subjects. This pattern holds true for French, German, and many other languages.

However, in Italian, while "Il parla" (he talks) is possible, it is more common to say "Parla" (talks) without an expressed subject: declarative sentences do not require subjects. The same is observed in Chinese, Arabic, and many other languages. This variability is termed the "pro-drop" parameter. In pro-drop languages like Italian and Chinese, the use of a subject is not mandatory, whereas in non-pro-drop languages such as English and German, subjects must always be included. This distinction, whether subjects are obligatory or optional in sentences, is an inherent characteristic of each language, classifying them as either pro-drop or non-pro-drop.

Learners whose native language follows a pro-drop pattern must reset the pro-drop parameter when learning a second language that adheres to a non-pro-drop structure. Similarly, those who speak a native language characterized by non-pro-drop features must undergo this adjustment when acquiring a second language that exhibits pro-drop characteristics.

Then, what is necessary for learners to reset this parameter? Within the framework of Universal Grammar (UG), two distinct responses have been proposed. The debate primarily centers on the necessity of negative evidence to facilitate this adjustment.

A significant number of linguists believe that, for a child to learn their first language, they only require positive evidence, exemplified by actual sentences. Similar to first language acquisition, Schwartz (1993) and some researchers argue that second language learners primarily rely on positive evidence, which eventually guides learners to adjust the parameter to adhere to the rules of the second language. Consequently, teachers should prioritize providing data that students can utilize to configure these parameters. In contrast, White (1991) and other colleagues contend that negative evidence is advantageous for second language learners because it highlights what is absent in the new language, facilitating the adjustment process. Despite these differing opinions regarding the role of negative evidence in second language learning, they all concur that the principles of Universal Grammar are not consciously learned.

While Universal Grammar (UG) theory is a linguistic approach, primarily focusing on first language (L1) acquisition, numerous scholars have tried to interpret second language (L2) learning using this framework. One of the most well-known theories is Krashen's Monitor Theory, which we will explore in the subsequent section.

Krashen's Monitor Model

Monitor Theory, developed by Stephen Krashen, is among the most important and recognized ideas in the field of second language acquisition (SLA). He developed his ideas in the late 1970s in a series of articles based on earlier research related to the natural acquisition of a first language. He further refined and expanded his theoretical framework in the early 1980s through a series of books (Krashen, 1982, 1983, 1985). Monitor Theory was the first theory to be developed specifically for SLA, paving the way for numerous research guidelines within the field. Its broad acceptance can be credited, at least in part, to its relevance and practicality in the everyday contexts of language learners and teachers.

Unlike behaviorism, Monitor Theory proposes a specialized model for second language learning. While Krashen does not overtly mention it, this theory appears to be related to Chomsky's viewpoint on language, which asserts that humans are uniquely endowed with a specific faculty for language acquisition. This implies that children already possess significant linguistic knowledge; they just require the triggering data in the input to activate this innate language ability. Krashen believes a similar mechanism is at play in SLA.

Within Monitor Theory, the comprehension of meaningful messages is the primary factor in language acquisition. The interactions of the linguistic information in those messages with the innate language acquisition faculty lead to SLA. According to Krashen, Monitor Theory offers insights into why what is taught is not always learned, why certain elements of a language are learned even if they are not taught, and how individual differences and various learning environments can lead to different outcomes in SLA. Krashen's theory is built on five core hypotheses:

1. The Acquisition-Learning Hypothesis
2. The Monitor Hypothesis
3. The Natural Order Hypothesis
4. The Input Hypothesis
5. The Affective Filter Hypothesis

The Acquisition-Learning Hypothesis

Krashen posits that acquisition and learning represent distinct pathways to acquiring knowledge. Once gained, these types of knowledge are stored separately. Acquisition occurs naturally and subconsciously, as learners interact naturally in their second language, prioritizing meaning over structure. In spontaneous language use, second language learners draw upon their acquired knowledge, guided by intuition rather than explicit rules. In other words, for Krashen, acquisition is identical in all important ways to the process children acquire their first language.

In contrast, learning entails gaining explicit understanding of language, encompassing its rules and structures – termed as "knowledge about language" by Krashen (1985, p. 1). Learning occurs when the second language (L2) is approached as a subject of study rather than utilized as the primary mode of communication. The process of gaining and using this knowledge involves conscious effort and intention.

The central and highly debated aspect of this differentiation lies in the notion that the two knowledge systems - namely, the acquired system and the learned system - remain entirely separate entities. Consequently, knowledge that is learned cannot be converted into acquired knowledge through practice and subsequently accessed for spontaneous use. This explains why learners may possess knowledge of rules yet struggle to apply them in spontaneous speech. Conversely, a learner might employ a grammatical structure correctly and instinctively but struggle to articulate the underlying rule. According to Monitor Theory, even if students grasp grammar rules through formal instruction, they cannot effectively employ that knowledge in spontaneous conversation since the rule has not been acquired.

Things to Consider 3.2

1. To what extent, do you agree with the Acquisition-Learning Hypothesis?
2. Do you have any personal learning experiences that can either validate or challenge the Acquisition-Learning Hypothesis?

The Monitor Hypothesis

Krashen emphasizes that learning and acquisition play specific roles in L2 performance. The Montor Hypothesis states that the sole function of learning is to act as a monitor or editor. Learning steps in only to polish the language structure after it has been produced by the acquired system. Fundamentally, acquired knowledge initiates what the speaker says, while learned knowledge serves to check and confirm its correctness.

Krashen believed that the role of learned knowledge as a monitor does not operate all the time. If learners are given sufficient time, and if focusing on the form is important, they may use this monitoring function, but only when they have consciously learned the relevant grammatical rule.

Things to Consider 3.3

1. Can you identify situations in which learners might make use of the monitor?
2. What could be examples of those who use the monitor too much ('over-users') or too little ('under-users')?
3. Considering the roles that the monitor plays in the Monitor Hypothesis, do you think that Krashen views the monitoring function as significant? Please provide reasons for your answer.

The Natural Order Hypothesis

Early research into both first and second language acquisition demonstrated that learners progress through specific sequences when acquiring particular forms like grammatical morphemes such as *-ing*, *-ed*, -s, and others. Moreover, they appear to pass through predictable stages in their learning of grammatical constructs such as questions and negation (Brown, 1973). These findings align with Krashen's Natural Order Hypothesis:

> We acquire the rules of language in a predictable order, some rules tending to come early and others late. The order does not appear to be determined solely by formal simplicity and there is evidence that it is independent of the order in which rules are taught in language classes. (Krashen, 1985, p. 1)

According to Krashen, these consistent patterns occur because all language acquisition is directed by the innate language acquisition faculty. In other words, the Natural Order Hypothesis reflects the universalism found in the theories of the 1970s, and it does not accommodate concepts such as language transfer and cross-linguistic influence.

Things to Consider 3.4

> Although some research has shown patterns in the development of certain language structures, Krashen's Natural Order Hypothesis has faced criticism. What could be the reason for this?

The Input Hypothesis

The input Hypothesis relates to the Natural Order Hypothesis by suggesting that progression in language development occurs when learners receive and process comprehensible input. *Comprehensible input* is defined as L2 input that is just beyond the learner's current L2 competence. If a learner's current competence is labeled as *i*, then comprehensible input is *i*+1, which is still understandable by the learner, but containing linguistic evidence relevant for the next step. Krashen believes that this type of input is the most crucial factor in second language acquisition (SLA).

Krashen explains that *roughly* tuned input will likely include various levels of input, including *i*, *i*+1, possibly *i*-1, *i*+2, and so on. If a teacher or a native speaker does not speak too rapidly or use overly complex language with a beginner, comprehensible input is likely guaranteed. Learners will naturally receive what they need, leading to spontaneous acquisition as long as they are exposed to this rich and comprehensible input. During this process, learners focus on meaning rather than form.

Things to Consider 3.5

1. After reviewing Krashen's statements below, consider his perspective on the significance of output and grammar teaching in second language acquisition (SLA).

   "Speaking is a result of acquisition and not its cause. Speech cannot be taught directly but emerges on its own as a result of building competence via comprehensible input."

   "If input is understood, and there is enough of it, the necessary grammar is automatically provided. The language teacher needs not attempt deliberately to teach the next structure along the natural order – it will be provided in just

> the right quantities and automatically reviewed if the student receives a sufficient amount of comprehensible input."
>
> (Krashen, 1985, p. 2)

2. Do you agree with Krashen's view on the role of output and grammar instruction in SLA? Why or why not?

Krashen emphasizes the significance of rich comprehensible input in his Input Hypothesis, asserting that it, coupled with the innate capacity for language acquisition, is fundamental to effective language acquisition. He contends that comprehensible input alone is not only a necessary condition for second language acquisition (SLA) but also a sufficient one. With clear, understandable input, SLA naturally follows as an inevitable outcome.

The Affective Filter Hypothesis

Krashen has claimed the essential role of the comprehensible input. However, it is also important that learners need to 'let that input in'. Krashen asserts that the Affective Filter plays this role. In other words, the Affective Filter determines how receptive a learner is to processing the input:

> Learners who are comfortable and have a positive attitude towards acquiring a language possess a lowered filter, enabling smooth access to comprehensible input. In contrast,

a stressful environment where learners feel uneasy elevates the affective filter, hindering their ability to process input. Krashen believes this filter can account for the variable outcome of SLA across L2 learners.

(Krashen, 1982, p. 31)

Things to Consider 3.6

Do you think emotional factors play a role in second language acquisition? Please elaborate on your response using your own experiences.

Contributions and Limitations of the Monitor Theory

Things to Consider 3.7

1. Which hypothesis(es) do you find most persuasive?
2. Which hypothesis(es) do you find least convincing?

Krashen's Monitor Model has faced challenges from various researchers. One of the issues questioned is whether or not learners have two separate systems. While Krashen argues that learned knowledge cannot be transferred into the acquired system, contrary evidence from numerous studies suggests otherwise. Both theoretical and empirical research highlight that with practice, learners can employ their learned second language skills spontaneously and without conscious effort (DeKeyser, 1998; Segalowitz, 2003). This implies that while learners may internalize information through different methods (implicit vs. explicit learning), the knowledge acquired through these different pathways is not entirely isolated.

Second, Krashen based his Natural Order Hypothesis on research related to English morpheme acquisition. Yet, there have been noted individual differences (e.g., learners' L1) in the order of acquisition (Goldschneider & DeKeyser, 2001), casting doubts on the robustness of the Natural Order Hypothesis.

The Input Hypothesis has also been questioned, particularly regarding the ambiguity surrounding the concept of *i*+1. To effectively examine this hypothesis, it is essential to clearly define the levels represented by *i* and *i*+1. Krashen (1982) vaguely suggested that language acquisition occurs when learners are exposed to material slightly above their current level of proficiency (*i*+1), aided by contextual or extralinguistic cues. He stressed the need for adequate input but did not clarify how to determine its sufficiency. While Krashen equates comprehension with acquisition, it is evident that understanding a story is not equal to acquiring linguistic structures there. One can comprehend a story without fully grasping its language rules. Gregg (1984) also expressed skepticism about how non-language context could help one understand specific language structures such as the third person singular –*s* or the formation of yes/no questions.

Although there have been many criticisms about the hypotheses that Krashen put forth, it is crucial to recognize the considerable impact the Monitor Model has made to the field of second language acquisition. This model has spurred a great deal of research and taken the field many steps forward. Krashen's ideas significantly influenced second language teaching during a time when instruction shifted from solely focusing on language forms, like memorizing rules or dialogues, to emphasizing meaning. Since then, meaning-focused instruction such as communicative language teaching and content-based instruction have become widely adopted. In addition, some research indicates that learners can make significant progress just from comprehensible input, without explicit instruction. However, it has also been shown that while comprehensible input is crucial, it alone is not enough for complete second language acquisition.

Things to Consider 3.8

Let's assume that you need to design English lessons as a teacher, drawing inspiration from Krashen's Theory. What elements would you incorporate and what would you exclude?

Moving forward, we will look into an instructional approach founded on Krashen's theory. Our objective is to assess whether the components you have previously identified are incorporated into this approach, recognized as the Natural Approach.

Natural Approach

Things to Consider 3.9

Based on Krashen's Monitor Model, the Natural Approach

was developed by Krashen and Terrell. In your understanding of the model, how would you define the term 'natural'?

Krashen and Terrell associated the Natural Approach with what they termed as 'traditional' language teaching methods. Traditional approaches are defined as "based on the use of language in communicative situations without recourse to the native language" (Krashen & Terrell, 1983, p. 9). The term 'natural' almost assumes that there are unnatural methods of learning a language. According to Krashen and Terrell, the unnatural methods encompass structural approaches, such as the grammatical method that breaks down a language into its constituent elements, and repetitive drills, such as listen-and-repeat exercises in classrooms. Consequently, the Natural Approach classroom strictly prohibits the use of these unnatural techniques.

Then, how does language learning occur in the Natural Approach setting? Students are not forced to verbalize words or expressions, let alone ensure accurate pronunciation. There is an absence of exhaustive exercises focusing on accurate usage, no emphasis on memorizing grammar rules or extensive vocabulary lists. The learning process is characterized by a relaxed and unhurried atmosphere. Through consistent exposure to the language in various contexts and by providing learners with meaningful and memorable input, akin to a child's interactions with their parents, speech naturally emerges without pressure or anxiety. In this approach, the acquisition of a second language occurs in a manner similar to the acquisition of a first language.

Now, let's explore the features of activities and materials compatible with the Natural Approach. As mentioned earlier, this approach prioritizes comprehensible input, meaningful communication, and fostering a relaxed classroom environment. According to Richards and Rodgers (2001), to reduce stress, learners are not pushed to speak until they feel prepared, but they are encouraged to engage with teacher commands and questions. The progression in activities moves gradually from "Yes/No" and straightforward display questions to more complicated and open-ended questions. Materials used in a natural approach classroom are designed to maximize the meaningfulness of activities and tasks, emphasizing comprehension and communication. Authentic materials, such as brochures or maps, along with visual aids and games, are used to facilitate language acquisition and encourage genuine understanding and communication.

The roles of learners evolve and progress throughout a Natural Approach course due to the various stages they must navigate. The initial stage is the pre-production phase, where learners have the freedom to decide when to start speaking without being compelled to respond orally. In the subsequent early-production stage, learners begin to articulate words, phrases, and simple sentences. They are expected to respond to straightforward questions and employ fixed conversational patterns. As they enter the speech-emergent stage, singular words and short phrases evolve into more extended expressions. Learners are encouraged to use complex utterances in role plays or games. Within this approach, the learner is described as "a processor of comprehensible input [who] is challenged by input that is slightly beyond his or her current level of competence and is able to assign meaning to this input through active use of context and extralinguistic information" (Richards & Rodgers, 2001, p. 186). Advancing to the fourth stage, the intermediate fluency stage, progress toward fluency persists with increased exposure to the language.

The teacher plays various crucial roles. First, they are responsible for consistently presenting comprehensible input in the target language and offering non-verbal cues. Second, creating a positive class environment that reduces emotional barriers is another key role. Lastly, the teacher makes decisions about classroom activities, group sizes, content, contexts, and materials.

As noted above, comprehension is key in the Natural Approach. Similar to this approach, Total Physical Response (TPR) is also grounded in the principle that comprehension comes first in language acquisition. In TPR, as the name implies, learners are not compelled to produce output; instead, they demonstrate their comprehension through actions. As they progress in their language development and become ready for production, output begins to play a role in the classroom. The comprehension-based approach is also known as the meaning-oriented approach.

The period from the early 1980s to the early 1990s saw a surge in the popularity of the meaning-oriented approach, with research confirming its beneficial impact on second language (L2) learning. Nevertheless, a great deal of research has indicated that focusing solely on comprehension in meaning-based instruction, while neglecting the importance of attention to form, is insufficient for second language (L2) learning. Cognitive approaches have laid the theoretical groundwork for these requirements, playing a role in shaping theories of second language (L2) learning that we will discuss in the next chapter.

Chapter Summary

When observing the development of children's language skills, we encounter numerous aspects that pose challenges for straightforward explanations. The seemingly effortless and innate nature of language acquisition in children leads us to embrace Chomsky's Universal Grammar theory. While this theory has been applied to understanding second language acquisition, as discussed in this chapter, there have been questions about its applicability. Krashen's Monitor Model attempts to explain second language acquisition while adhering to Chomsky's fundamental viewpoints. Although Krashen's model has had significant influence, it has also faced numerous criticisms. While Chomsky's Universal Grammar theory and the Monitor Model may be plausible for children's language acquisition, many second language learners, particularly adolescents and adults, find these theories less convincing in explaining their own L2 learning process. This does not render the approach meaningless or unhelpful; indeed, L2 learners, including adults, do acquire (Krashen's meaning of acquisition) their second language to some extent. However, given that the L2 learning process involves explicit learning to a significant degree, it is essential to consider how our conscious processes and explicit learning contribute to the overall L2 learning experience.

Chapter 4

Cognitive Approach to Instructed SLA

1. The Nature and Type of Second Language Knowledge

2. Information Processing Theory

3. Skill Acquisition Theory

4. Perspectives on Learner Language

5. Second Language Learning Theory within Cognitive Viewpoints

6. Teaching Approaches

7. Chapter Summary

Chapter 4

Cognitive Approach to Instructed SLA

Things to Consider 4.1

> From this viewpoint, second language acquisition (SLA) resembles the process of attaining complex skills, such as mastering a musical instrument or excelling in sports like tennis. How do you perceive this viewpoint? Do you agree or disagree, and what are your reasons for your stance?

The term 'cognition' originates from the Latin verb *cognoscere*, which translates to 'to get to know'. Cognition refers to how information is processed and learned by the human mind. Researchers in second language acquisition (SLA) have explored the factors involved in gaining a thorough understanding of an additional language to the extent that it can be used fluently for both comprehension and expression. In this chapter, we will study cognitive theories of second language acquisition that have been developed to explain how second language acquisition functions as a form of cognitive activity. To this end, the upcoming section will introduce fundamental terms and theories within the area of cognition.

The Nature and Type of Second Language Knowledge

Things to Consider 4.2

Reflect on your knowledge of your first language (L1) in comparison to your second language (L2). Are there similarities or differences?

Explicit and Implicit Knowledge

From a cognitive perspective, one way of explaining the knowledge that learners process regarding the second language (L2) is by categorizing it as either explicit or implicit knowledge (Rebuschat, 2013). The key distinction between these two lies in their level of consciousness. Explicit L2 knowledge has been described as knowledge that learners are aware of and can intentionally recall from memory. It is essentially 'knowledge about' the language. Learners are aware that they are dealing with this information, and they have the capacity to articulate it, whether in the form of an L2 rule or a description of how the L2 is used. While explicit knowledge does not always consist of technical terminology, learners may employ metalinguistic terms when expressing their explicit knowledge (Basturkmen, Loewen, & Ellis, 2002).

On the contrary, implicit L2 knowledge is referred to as 'knowledge of' the language rather than 'knowledge about' language. Implicit knowledge operates on an unconscious level. In other words, learners might not be fully aware that they have this knowledge, and they may not be able to put it into words (Ellis, 2005; Rebuschat, 2013). Implicit knowledge is like the innate understanding that native speakers have about their first language (L1), and this allows them to concentrate on conveying their intended message rather than the specific language structures needed for communication. Learners might characterize it as intuition or feeling.

L2 learners can possibly possess linguistic knowledge without being consciously aware of it, although this scenario is more common among those who acquire the language naturally as opposed to those who receive formal instruction. On the other hand, L2 speakers might have substantial explicit knowledge about the language but might not have corresponding levels of implicit knowledge. Furthermore, instructed L2 learners frequently exhibit greater levels of explicit and metalinguistic knowledge than do L1 speakers (Alderson & Hudson, 2013).

In terms of cognitive processing, learners need to use their attentional resources to retrieve explicit knowledge from memory. Consequently, the utilization of explicit knowledge necessitates cognitive exertion, and the time needed to access it prohibits rapid and spontaneous language production (Ellis, 2009). Conversely, learners can swiftly and unconsciously access implicit knowledge, enabling its application in spontaneous communication. While implicit knowledge is asserted to be the primary type of knowledge necessary for spontaneous communication, it is also recognized that language production generally involves a combination of implicit and explicit knowledge (Bialystok, 1982; Ellis, 2009).

Interface and Non-interface Position

Things to Consider 4.3

1. Which form of knowledge, explicit or implicit, do you believe is easier for learners to have in second language classrooms and why?
2. Do you believe that explicit knowledge learners have gained can turn into implicit knowledge?

In general, it is challenging to teach and gain implicit knowledge within L2 classrooms, particularly in EFL settings where conditions often favor of gaining explicit knowledge. The question of whether explicit knowledge acquired through instruction can lead to the development of the implicit knowledge essential for spontaneous L2 use has sparked considerable debate among SLA researchers (N. Ellis, 1993, 2007). Essentially, the discussion revolves around whether learners can attain explicit knowledge in class and expect it to transition into implicit knowledge. In other words, can learners gain explicit knowledge in the classroom, and then assume that it will turn into implicit knowledge? Or can implicit knowledge be gained only implicitly, while explicit knowledge remains explicit? Three positions have been proposed to address this question: non-interfacte, weak interface, and strong interface.

The non-interface position suggests that explicit and implicit knowledge are two distinct systems, asserting that explicit knowledge cannot transform into implicit knowledge (R. Ellis, 2009). This proposed incapacity of explicit knowledge to transition into implicit knowledge has implications for the classroom. If instructing explicit grammar rules merely results in explicit knowledge, which is mainly useful for applying rules in situations where learners have ample time to monitor their production, then there is limited value in teaching these rules if the instructional aim is to foster free communication in the L2. Advocates of the non-interface standpoint contend that providing learners with rich and plentiful input to engage in communication is the optimal pedagogical approach for L2 classrooms.

The weak interface stance claimed that while explicit and implicit knowledge remain separate, there exists a connection between the two and they work together during L2 production (N. Ellis, 2007). Furthermore, the weak interface perspective suggests that explicit knowledge aids in monitoring L2 production and enhances the probability that learners will recognize explicitly taught forms within the input.

Finally, the strong interface position which posits that explicit knowledge can be converted into implicit knowledge through ample practice. This main theoretical support for the strong interface position comes from Skill Acquisition Theory, which will be discussed in the following section.

Up to this point, we have considered the fundamental terms and concepts necessary for grasping the cognitive approach. In the upcoming sections, we will explore key theories associated with the cognitive approach.

Information Processing Theory

One of the well-known theories in the field of cognitive psychology is the information processing theory, which emerged during the 1970s. This theory is based on the idea that humans do not merely respond to stimuli from the environment. Instead, they actively engage in processing the information they receive. Within the framework of the information processing theory, attention plays an essential role. When we process new information, it necessitates our focused attention for proper processing. However, there is a limitation to our attentional capacity. If we use up all our attention on processing the new information, we become unable to process other incoming information, despite its abundance in our environment. Gradually, with experience and practice, once unfamiliar information becomes easier to process, allowing us to allocate our attention to additional incoming data. Using more technical terms, the initial stage of dealing with new information is referred to as *controlled processing*, which is a conscious and effortful process. Through practice, controlled processing gradually transitions into *automatic processing*, which demands small effort and take up few cognitive resources.

Language Learning and Information Processing Theory

Within the framework of information processing theory, the acquisition of a second language adheres to a comparable pattern of information processing as outlined earlier. Second language learners initially need to pay their attention to various aspects of the language they are trying to comprehend and use. However, there is a limit to how much information they can process, so they naturally prioritize understanding the key words in a message to grasp its meaning. They rarely pay much attention to the grammatical morphemes (e.g., *-ed*, -s, and *a/the*) attached to some words, especially when these do not significantly affect the overall meaning. Through experiences and practice, learners become able to understand it quickly and even automatically, which enables them to attend to other aspects of the language (e.g., language forms).

Automaticity and Restructuring

Automaticity stands out as a vital concept within the information processing framework. It is important to note that the term 'practice' here encompasses a broad range of activities, extending beyond mere mechanical drills and limited language production. Practice also includes extensive exposure to and comprehension of various aspects of the language.

Another important concept within information processing theory is *restructuring*. Restructuring refers to the self-reorganization of a learner's internal representation of grammatical knowledge. This takes place when qualitative changes occur in a learner's internal representation of the second language. Restructuring involves changes in knowledge that can be either large or small, sudden or gradual, but they always pertain to qualitative changes associated with progress or development. However, it is important to note that the concept of restructuring should not be equated with increased accuracy.

The view that development does not always mean increasing accuracy is clear in the notion of *U-shaped behavior*, which is destabilization as a consequence of restructuring. The process is defined as "the appearance of correct, or nativelike, forms at an early stage of development which then undergo a process of attrition, only to be reestablished at a later stage" (Sharwood Smith & Kellerman, 1989, p. 220). That is, U-shaped behavior illustrates three stages of linguistic development. In the initial stage, a learner correctly produces a particular linguistic form. In Stage 2, the learner seems to forget what they knew in Stage 1, producing the form incorrectly. Finally, in Stage 3, similar to Stage 1, the learner once again uses the form correctly. In a U-shaped learning pattern, the linguistic outcomes in the final stage (Stage 3) may appear indistinguishable from those in the initial stage (Stage 1), as both seem to resemble the target language. However, it is crucial to recognize that the underlying representations at Stage 1 and Stage 3 are qualitatively different. In the first stage, the correct use of the form is somewhat accidental, while in the final stage, accuracy is grounded in a comprehensive understanding of target-like functions and meanings.

Lightbown's 1983 study extensively examined U-shaped behavior observed in French learners of English within a classroom setting. The study focused on how these learners used the *-ing* form in English across the sixth, seventh, and eighth grades. In the sixth grade, when describing a picture, students correctly said, "He is taking a cake." However, in the seventh grade, when presented with the same picture, they responded with, "He take a cake," indicating an incorrect use of the *-ing* form.

The apparent decline in knowledge can be explained by Lightbown as follows: In the sixth grade, learners were introduced to the present progressive tense. Since this was their first encounter with this particular verb form in English, they associated it with the simple present tense in French, which had no equivalent counterpart. As a result, they not only used the present progressive correctly in situations where the *-ing* form was appropriate but also incorrectly overused it in contexts where the simple present tense was more suitable. When the simple present tense was introduced later on, learners had to grasp this new form while also reconfiguring their understanding of the present progressive. This process of adjustment and restructuring led to a decrease in both the use and accuracy of their language, a phenomenon referred to as back-sliding. However, once learners developed a solid grasp of both the present progressive and the simple present tense, they became capable of using the present progressive exclusively in contexts where it was appropriate. Lightbown (1985) provides the following rationale for restructuring:

> [Restructuring] occurs because language is a complex hierarchical system whose components interact nonlinear ways. Seen in these terms, an increase in error rate in one area may reflect an increase in complexity or accuracy in another, followed by overgeneralization of a newly acquired structure, or simply by a sort of overload of complexity which forces a restructuring, or at least a simplification, in another

part of the system. (Lightbown, 1985, p. 177)

Skill Acquisition Theory

Knowledge can also be categorized into declarative knowledge and procedural knowledge. This differentiation is used to refer to two different mental representations of knowledge in Skill Acquisition Theory. Declarative knowledge is the type of knowledge that learners can consciously recognize and express in words. On the other hand, procedural knowledge is automatized and available for use without awareness. In many respects, these terms align with explicit and implicit knowledge, respectively.

Skill acquisition theory posits that the process of learning, including language acquisition, begins with declarative knowledge. With continued practice, declarative knowledge transforms into procedural knowledge (i.e., understanding 'how'). The transition from declarative to procedural knowledge is referred to as proceduralization or automatization. In second language classrooms, learners first receive explicit explanations provided by their instructors or textbooks, and through practice, this knowledge can change into procedural or implicit knowledge.

Perspectives on Learner Language

From the cognitive perspective, learner language is perceived as a system governed by its own set of rules. This notion is encapsulated by the term *interlanguage*, coined by Selinker (1972). Interlanguage denotes the distinct language system that each learner constructs at any particular stage of their development. This concept underscores that learners' language should not be seen as deficient or characterized by random errors; instead, it should be recognized as a system in its own right (Gass & Selinker, 2008).

Interlanguage has elements of the native language and the target language. Furthermore, there are specific common traits observed across many interlanguage systems, such as the inclination to omit function words. Interlanguage is systematic but also dynamic, constantly developing as learners receive more input and revise their hypotheses about the target language. However, the journey of language acquisition does not consistently entail linear progression. Learners may undergo gradual or sudden improvements, but they may also encounter periods of plateau before further progress is stimulated. Selinker (1972) coined the term *fossilization* to characterize this phenomenon, which generally denotes the cessation of learning.

Since it is difficult to pinpoint the exact moment when learning stops, some researchers like Long (2003) suggest that it seems more appropriate to use the term *stabilization* of linguistic forms, rather than fossilization. In second language acquisition, it is common for learners to reach plateaus where their languages are far different from the norms of the target language. Furthermore, it seems that their interlanguage systems tend to become fossilized or stabilized, regardless of their efforts to expose themselves to more of the target language.

This leads to the natural question of what causes this phenomenon of fossilization or stabilization. A primary causal factor is the native language influence, but it is not the sole factor at play. Han (2004) noted that "fossilization is internally determined due to the constant functioning of maturational and native language constraints, yet it can be modulated (aggravated or alleviated) by environmental, social, and psychological forces" (p. 43).

Learner Errors

Until the late 1960s, the speeches of second language learners were regarded as incorrect versions of the target language. However, in cognitive perspectives, errors are no longer solely considered a result of imperfect learning; instead, they are regarded as insights into a learner's grasp of the second language. Errors are seen as "indications of a learner's attempt to figure out some system, that is, to impose regularity on the language the learner is exposed to" (Gass & Selinker, 2008, p. 102).

In tandem with the criticisms directed at the contrastive analysis hypothesis and the associated emphasis on the learner's language system, a new approach emerged for analyzing learner errors, known as *error analysis*. Error analysis is a type of linguistic analysis that focuses on the errors learners made. While contrastive analysis makes a comparison between the target language and the first language, error analysis compares the errors a learner makes when producing the target language with the correct forms of the target language itself. A number of studies were carried out in second language classrooms using error analysis, with the aim of providing instructional support and correction.

Error analysis mainly classifies the source of errors into two types, *interlingual errors* and *intralingual errors*. Interlingual errors are those that stem from the influence of the learner's first language, while intralingual errors arise from the specific language being learned. Intralingual errors do not have to do with learners' first language, and it can be expected that those errors occur from speakers of a wide range of first languages.

However, pinpointing the exact source of errors can often be challenging. Error analysis focuses on describing what learners actually do, rather than speculating on what they might do. It does not always provide clear insights into the reasons behind their errors.

Another major criticism of error analysis is directed to its heavy reliance on errors. In other words, error analysis is exclusively based on errors learners actually made. However, it is evident that learners often refrain from employing certain linguistic elements they find challenging (Schachter, 1974). This *avoidance* can result in the absence of specific errors. Without errors to analyze, assessing learners' interlanguage development becomes challenging.

In summary, cognitive approaches have brought about significant shifts in our understanding of learner language and have emphasized the considerable role of attention in second language acquisition. Influenced by these perspectives, numerous theories regarding second language learning have been put forth. Subsequent sections will present some of the key theories that have been influenced by cognitive viewpoints.

Second Language Learning Theory within Cognitive Viewpoints

In this section, we will study cognitive approaches that have provided theoretical underpinnings for second language classroom instruction. Of these approaches, particular attention will be paid to the interaction approach, which has held a pivotal role in the area of instructed second language acquisition (Adams, 2007).

Interaction Approach: Interaction, Negotiation for meaning, Output, and Noticing

Things to Consider 4.4

Consider a communication below. A and B are describing a railway station.

A: Platform two door is closed.

B: You mean the gate is closed?

A: Gates? Yeah, the gates are closed. Yeah, yeah, the gate is like the door.

B: Yeah, closed. The gate is closed.

(Bitchener, 2004, pp. 81-82)

1. What is happening in the conversation? Is 'negotiation for meaning' going on? If so, where?
2. Do you think L2 learning takes place in this conversation? Why or why not?

As discussed in Chapter 3, Krashen posited that comprehension is the pathway to learning, and that the more one comprehends, the more one learns. Long (1983) agreed with Krashen that comprehensible input is important. However, Long differed from the prevailing emphasis on input by highlighting the role of interaction. He proposed that the most beneficial comprehensible input for learners is the one that has been adjusted through interaction. The following example shows how input becomes more comprehensible through interaction.

(picture description)

Jane: All right now [reading from the script], above the sun place the squirrel.
He's right on the top of the sun.

Hiro: What is ... the word?

Jane: OK. The sun.

Hiro: Yeah, sun, but

Jane: Do you know what the sun is?

Hiro: Yeah, of course. Wh-what's the

Jane: Squirrel. Do you know what a squirrel is?

Hiro: No.

Jane: OK. You've seen them running around on campus.
They're little furry animals. They're short and brown

and they eat nuts like crazy.

(Adapted from Gass & Varonis, 1994, p. 296)

Long also asserted that when learners participate in meaningful interaction, they often discuss and clarify meanings. Specifically, if there is a misunderstanding because of linguistic difficulties, learners will attempt to resolve the misunderstandings by focusing on the problematic language aspects. This process of seeking clarity in communication (i.e., negotiation for meaning) helps learners notice language areas they struggle with, thus aiding the process of second language acquisition.

Let's consider another example.

NNS: The windows are crozed.
NS: The windows have what?
NNS: Crossed.
NS: Crossed? I'm not sure what you're saying here.
NNS: Windows are closed.
NS: Oh, the windows are closed. Oh, Ok.

(Pica, 1994)

In this conversation, the native speaker (NS) initially fails to understand the non-native speaker's (NNS) first statement, resulting in a request for further clarification. Despite the NNS's response of "crossed," the NS is still confused. The NNS makes another attempt to clarify, eventually achieving successful communication. While they are negotiating for meaning, the NNS acknowledges his problem and makes efforts to repair it for better understanding.

The following episode between a native speaker (NS) and a nonnative speaker (NNS) also shows how negotiation takes place and the excerpt from the interview with the NNS show this negotiation helps his understanding (Mackey, 2012):

> NNS: Does he has some hair?
> NS: He has a little bit of hair.
> NNS: A little bit? What do you mean a little bit?
> NS: He has twelve of them.
> NNS: He is twelve? What does it mean?
> NS: He has twelve hairs on his head.
> NNS: What does it mean he has twelve hair?
> NS: On his head he has one, two, three, four... twelve hairs
> NNS: OK

Excerpt from stimulated recall interview with the NNS in the episode above:

> So I asked her and she says a number and I still not understood so again I have ask her and this time she tell me by counting, she say one, two, three, four and so I see she is counting hair and little bit have mean small amount. It is good because when I ask her for her meaning, she can explain me, and then I can understand. First I think little bit maybe refer

sides of head, now I see mean little, few, only twelve, is not many. I think have we have thousand and thousand of hair on head but in this case have only little bit. Twelve. Few.

(Mackey, 2012, p. 132)

As we have seen above, when we communicate with others, we both express ourselves and take in information. Throughout this exchange, the conversation is adjusted, making the message clearer. This clarity is achieved not just through receiving modified input, but also through refining what we express. In a conversation, what one person puts out as input becomes the output for another.

Swain (1985, 1995) argued that clear and understandable expressions (i.e., comprehensible output) are just as crucial for second language acquisition as receiving clear and understandable input (i.e., comprehensible input). According to Swain, when learners produce language, they shift from focusing on meaning to structure. While understanding a message might not require deep analysis of its structure, expressing oneself demands careful attention to the way language is constructed, especially if the aim is to be clear. As Swain (1995) puts it, "learners ... can fake it, so to speak, in comprehension, but they cannot do so in the same way in production" (p. 127). In other words, they need to focus more on language structure when producing content.

Let's then consider the output generated during the process of negotiating meaning. When individuals engage in dialogue, misunderstandings may arise. In order to solve these, they may employ various strategies like asking for clarification (e.g., "Pardon me? Could you repeat that?"), seeking confirmation (e.g., "Are you asking if I'm available for you?"), and verifying comprehension (e.g., "Am I making sense to you?"). Let's reflect on the following episode:

NNS:	And in hand in hand have a bigger glass to see.
NS:	It's err. You mean, something in his hand?
NNS:	Like spectacle. For older person.
NS:	Mmmm, sorry I don't follow, it's what?
NNS:	In hand have he have has a glass for looking through for make the print bigger to see, to see the print, for magnify.
NS:	He has some glasses?
NNS:	Magnify glasses he has magnifying glass.
NS:	Oh aha I see a magnifying glass, right that's a good one, ok.

Excerpt from stimulated recall interview with the NNS:

> In this example I see I have to manage my err err expression because he does not understand me and I cannot think of exact word right then. I am thinking thinking it is nearly in my mind, thinking bigger and magnificate and eventually magnify. I know I see this word before but so I am sort of talking around around this word but he is forcing me to think harder, think harder for the correct word to give him so he can understand and so I was trying. I carry on talking until finally I

get it, and when I say it, then he understand it, me.

(Mackey, 2012, pp. 132-133)

In this episode, as they work towards achieving mutual understanding, they encounter communication barriers. The NNS continuously modifies his statements to ensure he is understood, striving for a satisfactory level of comprehension. When he adjusts his communication, as shown by his recall, he is compelling himself to think more intensively to produce clearer and more precise output. This kind of output is referred to as *modified output* or *pushed output*.

Learner output also serves as testing hypotheses that learners have about the L2 (Swain, 1995). If learners try out a form in their output and receive disconfirmation as to its accuracy (as in the aforementioned episode), either through communication breakdown or corrective feedback, they can have the opportunity to reassess their hypothesis. Conversely, learners may accept their hypothesis in the absence of any disconfirming sign. Thus, output is seen not as a mere result of learning, but rather as something that can contribute to L2 development.

In sum, during interactions aimed at negotiating meaning, learners aim to express themselves clearly and accurately, leading to the exchange of comprehensible input between interlocutors. Furthermore, while making output, learners notice what they know and what they do not know. This awareness facilitates their focus on incoming input, enabling them to seek necessary information. With appropriate corrections, they can also identify differences between their own utterances and the correct forms.

Teaching Approaches

Interactional approaches have played a significant role in the development of second language (L2) teaching methods. These methods are characterized by: (1) promoting meaningful interaction and language use, (2) achieving a balance between accuracy and fluency, (3) focusing on both form and meaning, and (4) acknowledging the importance of teacher feedback.

These elements are integrated into two main teaching approaches, Communicative Language Teaching (CLT) and Task-Based Language Teaching (TBLT). Numerous theoretical and empirical research findings have been reported about Communicative Language Teaching (CLT) and Task-Based Language Teaching (TBLT). However, due to the limitations of this book, only a concise overview of these two will be provided in the subsequent sections.

Communicative Language Teaching

The central goal of this approach is to foster communicative competence (Hymes, 1971), which refers to the ability to effectively use language in practical, real-world situations. Simply stated, the aim is to assist learners in becoming proficient language users by emphasizing the practical functions that language serves, such as seeking information or requesting permission. This approach encourages learners to actively engage in activities focused on meaning, leading to language acquisition (Brumfit, 1984). Communicative Language Teaching (CLT) is not a rigid method; it does not prescribe specific content, syllabi, or teaching techniques. CLT can be applied through various ways, but its main objective is the development of communicative competence.

Communicative Competence

Communicative competence is usually defined as the ability to understand and appropriately engage in social behaviors, requiring the learner's active involvement in using the target language (Canale & Swain, 1980). This includes four key competencies: linguistic competence (grammatical competence), pragmatic competence (sociolinguistic competence), discourse competence, and strategic competence.

Linguistic competence is concerned with understanding the language itself, encompassing its form and meaning. Specifically, it involves knowledge of spelling, pronunciation, vocabulary, word formation, grammatical structure, and linguistic semantics. Færch, Haastrup, and Phillipson (1984) emphasize that communicative competence is inseparable from linguistic competence, asserting that it is impossible to imagine someone as communicatively competent without a foundation in linguistic competence.

Pragmatic competence primarily involves the skill of using language to accomplish specific communicative purposes and intentions. To achieve this, students must understand the relationship between grammatical forms and functions and learn how to apply them appropriately in different situations.

Things to Consider 4.5

Let's assume that you say (a) and (b).

(a) If you'd wait a minute, I will see if Mr. Kim is able to talk to you.

(b) Hang on a minute. I'll get him.

1. What is the purpose behind your statement?
2. Can you identify the distinctions between (a) and (b)? (e.g., language forms, level of politeness, etc.)

Both sentences serve the same communicative purpose but vary in terms of politeness and formality, commonly referred to as *register*. The choice of sentence structures and vocabulary is influenced by the relationships between conversational partners. Learners possessing pragmatic competence can skillfully choose language that suits the social context, demonstrating their ability to navigate various social situations effectively.

Discourse competence includes a broad range of skills, including the ability to initiate, sustain, and advance conversations, manage discourse turns, and utilize cohesive devices in both written and spoken text. Achieving natural and successful communication requires language strategies for initiating, interrupting, and confirming in conversation. For instance, if a speaker intends to shift the topic, employing signals like 'by the way' becomes essential; failure to provide such cues may result in an awkward transition. Appropriate use of discourse markers contributes to the smooth flow of conversation. A similar competence is necessary for effective writing and reading. Proficiency in discourse allows second language learners to comprehend and apply suitable discourse markers. In the sentence "Some wines have 'proprietary' names. That is to say, their names were created by the producers," the second sentence serves as a restatement and explanation, with 'That is to say' linking the meanings. Discourse competence empowers learners to construct coherent texts or engage in cohesive conversations.

Strategic competence pertains to "how to cope in an authentic communicative situation and how to keep the communicative channel open" (Canale & Swain, 1980, p. 25). Essentially, strategic competence involves employing effective communication strategies when learners encounter difficulties expressing themselves or comprehending the interlocutor due to limitations in their second language resources.

Things to Consider 4.6

Consider the following conversation between a native speaker of English and a Korean student:

Student:	My uncle has jeonwonjutak.(Korean)
Native speaker:	What's that?
Student:	It's a house, not big, small, you know... in the country. It has a garden... (gestures a circle to show an area of surrounding land), you know.
Native speaker:	Oh, like a cottage, a country cottage.

1. What is happening here?

2. Have you found yourself in a situation similar to that of the student? How do you cope with the case?

In this example, the student does not know the word 'cottage' and resorts to using Korean. Initially, she code-switches to Korean and subsequently employs paraphrase, assisted by gestures, demonstrating an effort to express her thoughts while compensating for her limited proficiency in English.

The mentioned episode provides just a glimpse of communication strategies, which can be implemented in various other forms. Dörnyei (1995) outlines the types of compensatory strategies as follows:

Compensatory Strategies

1. Circumlocution: Describing or exemplifying the target object of action (e.g., a small mat you put under a cup for a coaster)
2. Approximation: Using an alternative term which expresses the meaning of the target lexical item as closely as possible (e.g., birds for sparrows)
3. Use of all-purpose words: Extending a general, empty lexical item to contexts where specific words are lacking (e.g., thing and stuff)
4. Word coinage: Creating a non-existing L2 word based on a supposed rule (e.g., vegetarianist, firstly)
5. Prefabricated patterns: Using memorized stock phrases, usually for "survival" purposes (e.g., Where is the...?)

6. Nonlinguistic signals: Mime, gesture, facial expression, or sound imitation
7. Literal translation: Translating literally a lexical item, idiom, compound word, or structure from L1 to L2 (e.g., cow meat)
8. Foreignizing: Using a L1 word by adjusting it to L2 phonology (i.e., with a L2 pronunciation) and/or morphology (e.g., adding to it a L2 suffix)
9. Code-switching: Using a L1 word with L1 pronunciation
10. Appeal for help: Asking for aid from the interlocutor either directly (e.g., What do you call...?) or indirectly (e.g., rising intonation, pause, eye contact, puzzled expression)
11. Stalling or time-gaining strategies: Using fillers or hesitation devices to fill pauses and to gain time to think (e.g., well, now let's see, uh, as a matter of fact)

(Adapted from Dörnyei, 1995, p. 58)

Compensatory strategies are not limited to the strategies listed above. Any efforts made by learners to sustain communication are regarded as communication strategies.

The primary objective of CLT is to facilitate learners in becoming proficient language users in authentic social settings, underscoring the significance of acquiring proper communicative competence to attain this goal.

Task-Based Language Teaching

In task-based language teaching (TBLT), lessons are designed based on the language skills needed to accomplish particular tasks, as opposed to focusing on language components like grammatical structures and vocabulary. In this approach, tasks serve as the primary unit of analysis, aligning with learners' practical needs in real-world situations. A task in this context mirrors activities that learners engage in outside the classroom, and task-based instruction aims to integrate these real-life tasks into the learning environment (Ellis, 2003). There are various features that a task should possess.

Nunan (2005) draws a distinction between a practical or real-world task (reflecting learners' language usage in real life) and a pedagogical task (what learners do in class). Real-world tasks are designed to emphasize the skills essential for learners to deal with real-life scenarios, often serving as the ultimate objective of a lesson or unit. Conversely, pedagogical tasks are designed as a bridge between the classroom and the real world, aiming to equip students with the language proficiency needed for real-life situations. Nunan (2005) provides the following definition for a task:

> A piece of classroom work that involves learners in comprehending, manipulating, producing or interacting in the target language while their attention is focused on mobilizing their grammatical knowledge in order to express meaning and in which the intention is to convey meaning rather than to manipulate form. The task should also have a sense of

> completeness, being able to stand alone as a communicative act in its own right with a beginning, middle and an end.
>
> (Nunan, 2005, p. 4)

According to Nunan, when students engage in and complete a task, they utilize information they have previously learned and integrate it with new information received during the task. This process ultimately leads to language learning. Linking tasks to real-life situations enables learners to use language meaningfully and serves as a trigger for learner motivation.

Incorporating real-life situations underscores the significance of recognizing learner needs within the framework of TBLT. Given that various learners have distinct learning requirements, they may need to apply the target language in diverse situations. Consequently, needs analysis not only informs the goals but also guides the development of pedagogical activities in the classroom.

In summary, the Interaction Approach underscores the importance of input, interaction, and output in language learning. Consequently, both CLT and TBLT advocate for learner interaction and communication. As we all know, communication does not take place in a vacuum. Therefore, a significant amount of research in this field has focused on the tasks or activities that learners and their interlocutors engage in to facilitate communication. Furthermore, various factors can influence the extent of interaction. It is crucial for teachers and educators to recognize these factors when implementing the Interaction Approach in the classroom.

Factors Influencing Interaction

In order to examine the optimal conditions for learning L2 during interaction, many researchers have investigated variables affecting interaction, and they have found three main factors that could influence interaction: (a) task characteristics, (b) interlocutor characteristics, and (c) contextual characteristics.

Task Characteristics

Communicative activities enable learners to participate in meaningful interaction. These meaning-focused activities are referred to as tasks. A task has the following features: (a) it resembles a real-world activity, (b) it has a primary focus on meaning, (c) it has a non-linguistic outcome, and (d) learners are expected to use their own linguistic resources (Ellis, 2003).

Things to Consider 4.7

Let's consider if the following activity meets the criteria for a task.

Activity: Finding the best route

You are traveling in New York City with your friend, and you've just arrived at Grand Central Station. You want to visit the Metropolitan Museum of Art. You have a map of the city and a subway and bus schedule. You need to determine the best route from the station to the museum.

(1) Is this similar with real-world activities?

(2) Is this mainly meaning-focused?

(3) Does this have an outcome?

Tasks can take various types. One of the features that can decide the type of task pertains to how the information in the task is presented to the learners (Pica, Kanagy, & Falodun, 1993). In a two-way information gap task, different pieces of information are assigned to different learners, requiring them to share data to complete the task. Conversely, in a one-way information task, one learner has all of the information and must convey it to the other individuals in the group. Alternatively, there can be situations where all learners are given the same information, leading to no information gap (Doughty & Pica, 1986).

Another aspect that defines a task is its expected outcome (Ellis, 2003). Tasks that necessitate learners to agree on a particular result are termed as having a convergent goal. On the other hand, tasks that allow learners to voice their individual perspectives without needing consensus are labeled as having a divergent goal. Researchers have found that involving learners in two-way information gap tasks in which they are required to agree on the outcome (convergent goal) is better for bring about more interaction and negotiation for meaning (Ells. 2003; Yilmaz, 2011).

Things to Consider 4.8

1. Can you evaluate the activity 'Finding the best route' on (a) the distribution of information and (b) the end result?
2. How might you modify 'Finding the best route' to bring about more interaction?

Interlocutor Characteristics

The individual with whom the learner is interacting, known as the task interlocutor, can influence the interaction. Research has explored various interlocutor types, such as native speakers, teachers, and L2 learners with similar, higher, or lower proficiency levels (Leeser, 2004; Sato & Ballinger, 2012). Given the limited opportunities for learners to interact with native speakers in L2 classrooms, except for their teachers who are native speakers, research into interaction among learners appears to be of particular interest to teachers.

Peer interaction, or interaction among learners, can occur in diverse patterns. The first variation involves different levels of proficiency, where learners interact with peers of higher, lower, or similar proficiency levels. The second variation pertains to differences in learner characteristics, with some being more passive and others more active or dominant during collaborative tasks (Kim & McDonough, 2008; Storch, 2002). Numerous studies have explored the impact of pair dynamics on task performance, yet a definitive conclusion has not been reached, leading to diverse outcomes.

Drawing on previous research, a reasonable suggestion is that maintaining a balance of power within pairs is crucial. For example, pairs in which one learner takes a dominant role and the other takes a passive one may not engage in much interaction if the more active one is doing most of the talking and task activities, while the other learner makes minimal contribution. Similarly, when both learners take a dominant role, there may be limited interaction as each individual is occupied in their own tasks, without actively listening or engaging with the other person. Thus, it is essential to assign distinct roles or offer clear instructions that facilitate an equal contribution from all learners in the task.

Likewise, learners will experience advantages through varying proficiency dynamics when there is a well-maintained balance of power. Learners engaged in relationships where one is an expert (higher proficiency) and the other is a novice (lower proficiency) may have beneficial interaction, as the expert aids the novice in enhancing their communicative skills throughout the task. Likewise, two novices may be able to work together to try to resolve their interactional difficulties.

The optimal peer dynamics remain uncertain. However, Ohta (2001)'s statement provides insight into why collaboration could be significant, irrespective of the characteristics of the peers involved: "[N]o learner is universally more or less capable than a peer, but that each learner presents an array of strengths and weaknesses that may be complementary" (p. 76). In other words, when learners engage in collaborative dialogue, they may pool these strengths and weaknesses, which co-construct more knowledge as a group than any of the individuals would construct on their own.

Contextual Characteristics

Second language (L2) learners typically engage in classroom interactions, which clarifies why research on L2 conducted in a controlled laboratory environment appears to lose its generalizability (Loewen & Nabei, 2007). L2 classroom environments vary in numerous ways (e.g., ESL vs. EFL, refer to

Chapter 1), leading to diverse experiences and outcomes in L2 learning.

Another context that is receiving increased attention for interaction research is computer-mediated communication (CMC) (Blake, 2000; O'Dowd, 2011). CMC refers to the activities involving the creation, exchange, and perception of information using a variety of networked communication applications (Romiszowski & Mason, 2013). CMC's capacity to connect individuals from different locations offers the potential to provide learners with linguistic input and interaction opportunities that were previously inaccessible (Pasfield-Neofitou, 2012).

Of particular interest from an interactive perspective is synchronous CMC (SCMC). This form of interaction occurs in real-time as participants communicate with each other either verbally or in written form through the computer. In terms of written SCMC, several benefits have been reported. One advantage is that it facilitates a slower communication process, potentially allowing learners to focus more on the accuracy of their language production. The reduced pace of interaction could also provide more time for learners to tap into their explicit knowledge while attempting L2 production. Additionally, written SCMC creates a written record, enabling learners to review and compare their errors with the target forms provided in any corrective feedback (Smith, 2009).

Synchronous computer-mediated communication (SCMC) can also be applied to verbal exchanges, either with or without accompanying video (Bueno-Alastuey, 2013). Notably, video-based SCMC shares more similarities with face-to-face interaction than its written counterpart. Unlike written

SCMC, the exploration of verbal SCMC has been limited. However, since the onset of the Covid-19 pandemic in 2020, there has been a growing interest among researchers in this area. Although its advantages over face-to-face interaction have not been definitively established, some studies suggest that regular use of SCMC may help reduce learner anxiety and can offer learners with opportunities for communication with native speakers (Abraham, 2008).

Chapter Summary

Cognitive theories highlight the significance of attention in the learning process, including language acquisition. Advocates of cognitive approaches believe in the efficacy of explicit learning and knowledge. Consequently, unlike Krashen's Monitor Model, L2 researchers within the cognitive framework, advocate either a weak interface position or a strong interface position. Within this perspective, acquiring explicit knowledge of the second language is seen as beneficial and even indispensable, respectively. In the context of second language processing, learners are encouraged to be aware of what they are learning and the problems they encounter. This awareness and problem-solving is effectively stimulated during interactive communication, where negotiation processes force learners to modify their output and recognize existing problems. This heightened awareness of problems prompts learners to actively seek information necessary for resolution, creating a self-reinforcing cycle.

Cognitive approaches offer a robust theoretical basis for L2 classroom teaching, particularly in EFL settings with adolescent and adult learners. Instructed SLA has evolved by incorporating numerous cognitive perspectives. In the subsequent two chapters, we will explore the evolution of L2 instruction and explore the latest prevailing approach.

Chapter 5

Approaches to Second Language Instruction

Chapter 5

Approaches to Second Language Instruction

In the preceding chapters, we explored prominent theories of second language (L2) learning and the corresponding instructional methods. The evolution of L2 teaching approaches is intricately linked to shifts in dominant L2 learning theories and the evolving requirements of learners in their pursuit of L2 learning. This chapter explores the transformation and progression of L2 instructional approaches, drawing comparisons between past and current trends. Particularly, we will examine three specific aspects: focus on forms, focus on meaning, and focus on form.

Focus on Forms vs. Focus on Meaning

Things to Consider 5.1

1. Reflecting on your second language learning experience, how did you learn?
2. Considering the terms, can you infer the meanings of 'focus

on forms' and 'focus on meaning'? Additionally, how did you go about learning a second language (focus on meaning or focus on forms)?

The conventional way of language instruction has long involved teachers and syllabus designers initially focusing on the analysis of the target language structure. This typically entails adopting an established analysis, often in the form of a pedagogical grammar or textbook, that is, what Wilkins (1976) termed the synthetic approach. Based on the analyses, the second language (L2) is broken down into components such as words, collocations, grammar rules, phonemes, intonation, and stress patterns. The elements identified in this process are subsequently sequenced for presentation as models to learners in linear fashion according to the criteria such as frequency and difficulty (usually intuitively assessed). Synthetic syllabi, particularly the prevalent structural syllabus, continue to be employed in classrooms worldwide. These syllabi involve the presentation of information about the L2 through both inductive and deductive approaches, leading to lessons that emphasize a focus on formS.

In this approach, the emphasis lies on teaching isolated grammatical forms in a decontextualized manner. The belief is that learners can subsequently incorporate these isolated forms for effective communication. The Grammar Translation Method (GTM) exemplifies this focus on forms. Under this method, students are required to possess a comprehensive understanding of grammatical rules and demonstrate the ability to translate texts between the L2 and the native language (L1).

Another example of the focus on forms is the Audiolingual Method (ALM), emerging from two prominent theories influential in the 1950s: behaviorist psychology (see Chapter 2) and structural linguistics. Structural linguistics perceives language as a system of hierarchical units, directing its inquiry towards linguistic elements like sounds, words, clauses, and so forth. This perspective heavily influences ALM, where grammatical structures take precedence over vocabulary, and accuracy is prioritized over fluency. Grounded in behaviorism, this approach sees all learning as a result of habit formation, and habits are believed to be formed through a process of memorization, repetition, and reinforcement. Consequently, ALM aims to instill L2 habits akin to those of native speakers using stimulus-response techniques involving repetition and pattern drills.

Both the Grammar Translation Method (GTM) and the Audiolingual Method (ALM) underscore the significance of instructing discrete grammar rules. However, by the late 1970s, it became evident that the focus on forms approach lacked effectiveness in facilitating learners' communication skills (Larsen-Freeman & Anderson, 2011). This led to the emergence of a purely communicative approach that regarded the teaching of grammar as undesirable. Educators were persuaded that grammar instruction was outdated and best avoided. This shift was reinforced by scholars like Krashen (1982; 1985), who asserted that teaching grammar had minimal impact on learners' L2 development (see Chapter 3). Instead, they advocated an instructional approach that prioritizes exposing learners to ample meaningful input, known as the focus on meaning. This approach operates on the belief that learners acquire a language inductively, grasping its underlying grammar through exposure to abundant meaningful L2 input.

The Natural Approach and French immersion programs exemplify the application of the focus on meaning approach. The Natural Approach was originally shaped by Terrell, a California-based Spanish teacher, with the goal of creating a teaching style grounded in the insights from naturalistic studies of second-language acquisition. Terrell collaborated with Krashen (see Chapter 3) to further refine the method's theoretical underpinnings. The approach aims to facilitate the natural acquisition of language within a classroom context, prioritizing communication and minimizing the significance of conscious grammar study and explicit correction of student errors. Additionally, efforts are made to cultivate a low-stress learning environment. In the Natural approach, language output is not forced, but it emerges spontaneously after students have been exposed to substantial amounts of comprehensible input. In Canadian French immersion programs, students engage in the study of subjects like mathematics, science, and history exclusively in the second language, which is French. Consequently, they are exposed to a substantial amount of meaningful input throughout the entire program.

Focusing on meaning approach emphasizes engaging in activities that focus on conveying meaning without giving any attention to linguistic forms. This approach gained significant popularity for prioritizing meaningful input and teaching substantive content over language form. Nonetheless, there were drawbacks associated with this method.

Research on French immersion programs in Canada has revealed that, despite receiving meaningful input in classrooms for several years, students encountered challenges with certain aspects of grammar. Specifically, these students demonstrated strong receptive skills in listening and reading; however, their productive skills in speaking and writing lacked grammatical accuracy in fundamental linguistic forms such as gender agreement and the use of tense markers. The difficulties observed in their language production could be linked to the shortcomings of the focus on meaning approach, as it did not prompt learners to actively notice certain grammatical aspects that, even if inaccurately expressed, did not impede the overall conveyance of meaning.

Unquestionably, producing inaccurate linguistic forms might not pose a problem, particularly when successful communication of meaning is achieved. The concern is learners may be misled into believing that their output is accurate, which potentially leads to the persistence of those inaccuracies (i.e., fossilization). Moreover, classrooms centered on meaning failed to provide learners with ample chances to produce their own output and receive corrective feedback on their second language (L2) production. Towards the end of the 1980s, it became increasingly evident that learners required not only meaningful input but also opportunities to actively produce output, enabling them to consciously recognize some of their linguistic problems (refer to Chapter 4).

The focus on meaning gained significant popularity in the 1980s. However, its drawbacks within French immersion programs and the growing recognition of the crucial role of learner noticing in second language (L2) learning have prompted a reassessment of the significance of instruction for language forms (Lee & VanPatten, 2003).

Focus on Form

Second language researchers and teachers have observed that L2 instruction exclusively focusing on either language forms (focus on forms) or meaning (focus on meaning) alone is not effective in helping learners reach the desired levels of communicative competence (achieving both accuracy and fluency). To address this, one approach to foster both fluency and accuracy is the concept of 'focus on form,' as proposed by Long (1991; 1996). Focus on form aims to overcome the limitations of both approaches by directing learners to pay attention to linguistic forms within the context of meaningful communication. This approach necessitates learners' involvement in activities centered around meaning before focusing on linguistic forms. The underlying assumption is that it is possible to integrate a form-focused element without disrupting the meaningful communication process (Lightbown & Spada, 1990). The interest in focus on form has grown since its inception and is now considered a prominent paradigm in second language acquisition research, bridging the gap between theory and practical application (Han, 2008). Therefore, in the following chapter, there will be a detailed discussion on focus on form, along with the provision of practical tips for classroom application.

Chapter Summary

The evolution of L2 instructional methods is not only shaped by language learning theories but is also closely tied to the growing needs and goals of language learners. Essentially, the shift in L2 instructional approaches mirrors the changing needs of learners. Moreover, this transformation highlights that an approach's strengths might transform into weaknesses when overemphasized without maintaining a balance. Focus on form has become increasingly popular as it harmonizes meaning and linguistic forms by integrating the strengths of prior approaches and offering resolutions to their problems.

Chapter 6

Focus on Form

1. Theoretical Underpinnings and Characteristics of Focus on Form

2. Pedagogical Application: Types of Focus on Form

3. Chapter Summary

Chapter 6

Focus on Form

Focus on Form now stands out as a significant paradigm that serves as a connection between theory and practical implementation. In this chapter, we will study Focus on Form in depth, examining both its theoretical underpinnings and its application in pedagogy.

Theoretical Underpinnings and Characteristics of Focus on Form

The primary theoretical concern of focus on form is how attention to both meaning and form can be combined to generate an optimal learning environment. In Long's (1991) original version of focus on form, he explicitly states that the change in attention (from attention to meaning to attention to language form) is prompted by an issue, such as an error committed by the learner: "Focus on form . . . overtly draws students' attention to linguistic elements as they arise incidentally in lessons whose overriding focus is on meaning or communication" (Long, 1991, pp. 45-46). This definition suggests that Long initially conceived of focus on form as a response to a learner's grammatical problems. Consequently, his notion of focus on form is constrained to an incidental or reactive focus on form, typically manifested through a teacher providing feedback in reaction to a learner's errors. However, as numerous studies have demonstrated that the impact of incidental focus on form on second language (L2) acquisition is constrained (Doughty,2003), the scope of the term 'focus on form' has been broadened to encompass a more comprehensive viewpoint, no longer limited only to incidental responses to learner problems.

In the present, the term 'focus on form' can take place in two ways - either spontaneously, reacting to immediate needs (referred to as reactive focus on form), or pre-emptively, with a proactive approach. The proactive focus on form involves the purposeful targeting of particular linguistic structures predetermined by the teacher, anticipating potential problems that students might encounter with specific grammatical constructs (Doughty & Williams, 1998).

Ellis (2001) has made a similar distinction between incidental focus on form and planned focus on form. Incidental focus on form is not predetermined and does not involve the pre-selection of specific target forms (akin to reactive focus on form). It responds to various linguistic forms as they emerge, addressing a diverse range of forms based on immediate needs. In contrast, planned focus on form entails prior preparation and the deliberate selection of target forms (similar to proactive focus on form). This approach involves the concentrated and repetitive targeting of one or two specific forms.

Whether one adopts a reactive or proactive approach to form, a crucial theoretical underpinning for focus on form is the concept of noticing. As discussed in the preceding chapter, learners have limited attentional resources, making it challenging to simultaneously focus on both meaning and form during communication (VanPatten, 1996). Generally, learners prioritize understanding the semantic content of an utterance (meaning) over morphosyntactic elements (form), as the primary goal of most interaction is mutual understanding with interlocutors and effective self-expression. Due to the tendency to prioritize meaning, learners frequently overlook or fail to pay attention to morphosyntactic information (form) in the input, especially when such information is redundant or not salient (for example, the third person *-s* in English present tense). The argument for focus on form, then, is that learners need to notice linguistic forms in order to acquire them (Leow, 2007; Schmidt, 1990, 1995). This reasoning brings us to the question of how learners can be directed to specific linguistic forms within the focus on form framework. The rest of this section will address this issue.

Pedagogical Application: Types of Focus on Form

Given that the goal of focus on form is to combine attention to meaning and form, it is important to consider the way in which this may be done in the classroom. This is closely related to the degree of explicitness. In other words, learner attention to form can be done either in an implicit way or in an explicit way.

An implicit way involves an indirect emphasis on linguistic structure, aiming to minimize disruptions to the conveyance of meaning and to avoid discussing grammar or language usage explicitly. Alternatively, there may be occasions where it becomes necessary to draw learners' attention more directly, either through explanations of grammar rules or by encouraging students to actively seek out these rules. This represents a more overt form of focus on form. The various techniques for focus on form can be positioned along a spectrum, ranging from implicit to explicit approaches, as illustrated in Figure 6.1.

Figure 6.1 Degree of Explicitness of Focus on Form Techniques

	Implicit (Unobtrusive) ---------------- Explicit (Obtrusive)					
Input flood	X					
Input enhancement		X				
Negotiation		X				
Recasts			X			
Dictogloss				X		
Text reconstruction					X	
Reformulation					X	
Consciousness raising tasks					X	
Processing instruction						X

(adapted from Doughty & Williams, 1998, p. 258)

As shown in Figure 6.1, techniques situated towards the implicit side are indirect approaches that do not disrupt meaningful communication as much as those positioned towards the explicit side, which are more disturbing and have the potential to interrupt meaningful communication. The focus on form techniques outlined in Figure 6.1 will be addressed and discussed in the following section.

One frequently used way for categorizing focus on form involves distinguishing between input-based and output-based approaches. Input-based techniques draw learners to attend to language form during processing of language input, whereas output-based techniques lead learners to attend to form during producing of language output.

Input-Based Techniques

In input-based techniques, learners attend to specific language forms as they encounter language input. The rationale behind this method lies in the recognition that learners may not equally notice all features in the second language (L2) input. For features that might not be easily noticed during the processing of L2 input, teachers need to assist learners in recognizing these aspects. One way to enhance the noticeability of L2 input is by increasing its perceptual salience, which can be achieved through techniques such as input flooding or input enhancement.

Input Flood

Input flood is the most implicit type of focus on form technique. As the term suggests, teachers present learners with numerous examples of the target form. The underlying assumption is that frequent exposure to the target form will increase its salience, and thereby draw the learners' attention to it (Loewen, Erlam, & Ellis, 2009).

To implement an input flood activity, first, the teacher should choose the target form(s) and then create or select a reading or listening text that contains abundant examples of the chosen target form(s). An example activity is presented below.

[Input Flood Example 1]

Activity: A Mysterious Letter. While investigating the murder of a Russian woman, the detective finds the following letter in the victim's apartment. The first paragraph of the letter appears to be missing. Read the letter and answer the questions the follow:

I will leave tomorrow. I will move to another city. I will change my name, color of my hair. I will become a completely different person. You won't recognize me. No one will recognize me. I will start a new life, find a new job, and new friends. My life will settle down gradually, and I will stop thinking about you. And I will be happy.

Help the detective solve his case by answering the following questions:

1. What is the author of this letter planning to do?
2. What do you think happened between the author of the letter and its addressee?
3. According to the author, how will the addressee react to her leaving?
4. Do you think the addressee of this letter could be a

suspect in the murder case? Why or why not?

[Input Flood Example 2]

The teacher has told me that I have homework today. It will have to be completed by tomorrow. I have looked at it, and it looks very difficult. I have asked my brother if he has ever worked on homework like this. He has never seen an assignment like this before. This will be the first time that I have needed help!

Questions for discussion

1. Has anything like this ever happened to you as a student?
2. What do you think the problem with the student's homework has been?
3. Do you think homework is useful?

(Adapted from Wong, 2005, p. 99-100)

The teacher can make an original text for input flooding or select a suitable excerpt from a textbook. Additionally, authentic materials like well-known songs, poetry, or book passages can be used. Songs, in particular, are ideal for input flooding due to their inherent linguistic patterns.

When employing the input flood technique, teachers need to be aware that students may not always recognize the use of the target form within the input. Learners tend to primarily attend to the sematic content of the input. Consequently, they tend not to notice non-salient and redundant morphosyntactic forms in the input (i.e., features with low communicative value) (Han, Park, & Combs, 2008). It is also possible that elevating the frequency of the target form may not noticeable enough for the learners. In such cases, an alternative focus on form technique, slightly more explicit than input flood, can be employed, as illustrated in the following section.

Input Enhancement

Input enhancement is a type of implicit focus on form technique similar to input flood. But input enhancement is considered as a slightly more explicit way compared to input flood in that the target form is highlighted in some way (Sharwood Smith, 1991, 1993). In many cases, the input enhancement occurs with written language, with the enhanced forms being bolded, underlined, put in a different font size, or highlighted in other way (i.e., textual enhancement). It is possible to enhance oral input by adding stress or by repeating the target form.

When employing an input enhancement technique in the L2 classroom, similar to input flood, the teacher selects the form(s) to focus on, creates and chooses relevant text. It is important to note that the target form(s) are highlighted. Nassaji and Fotos (2011) propose the following stages for creating textually enhanced texts.

Steps:

1. Select a specific grammar point that the students find challenging.
2. Highlight that form in the text using one or two enhancement

techniques such as boldfacing only or boldfacing and italicizing.

3. Limit the target feature to a single linguistic form. Highlighting various forms can distract the learners' attention and hinder them from making precise form-meaning connections.
4. Employ comprehension strategies to ensure that learners remain focused on understanding the meaning.
5. Avoid offering metalinguistic explanations.

As pointed out in Step 4, it is crucial for students to engage in reading the text with a focus on meaning. To facilitate this, teachers should employ strategies that effectively maintain students' attention on meaning. Achieving this goal can involve incorporating diverse post-reading activities. An example activity of input with enhancement is presented in the examples below.

[Input Enhancement Example 1]

In my family, everybody collects something. My sister likes to collect pieces of clothing such as a **scarf**. She has **scarves** of different colors in her collection. She also likes to collect pictures of animals. Sometimes you can see one **wolf** or many **wolves** in the picture. She does not have only one **shelf** filled with pictures but five **shelves**. My younger brother likes to collect **leaves**. He likes to pick out his favorite **leaf** on the ground during fall.

(text continues)

Questions:

1. Do you have a collection? What about members of your family?
2. What does the author's sister like to collect?
   (questions continue)

[Input Enhancement Example 2]

The teacher **has told** me that I have homework today. It will have to be completed by tomorrow. I **have looked** at it, and it looks very difficult. I **have asked** my brother if he **has** ever **worked** on homework like this. He **has** never **seen** an assignment like this before. This will be the first time that I **have needed** help!

This text is provided as an example of input flood, which can be used to enhance the target form through input enhancement.

Consciousness-Raising Task

A consciousness-raising task is another input-based focus-on-form technique that is frequently used in L2 classrooms. The concept of 'consciousness-raising' generally means to increase awareness about a particular subject. Within second language acquisition (SLA), Rutherford and Sharwood Smith (1985) initially coined the term to describe efforts aimed at directing L2 learners' attention to the structural features of the target language.

Grammar consciousness-raising (GCR) tasks aim to increase learners' awareness of the rules governing specific language forms while providing them with opportunities to engage in meaningful interaction. Essentially, these tasks seek to help learners develop explicit knowledge about how the target language works and to encourage them to negotiate meaning. The underlying theoretical foundation is that explicit understanding of grammar structures aids learners in noticing those forms in subsequent communicative input (Ellis, 1990; Nassaji & Fotos, 2004) and that interaction plays a vital role in language acquisition (Ellis, 1990, 2003). Utilizing tasks and group activities that require negotiating meaning can expose learners to more comprehensible input (Long, 1991) and push them to refine their own output through interaction (i.e., pushed output or modified output). It is important to point out that in GCR tasks, learners are not given explicit information about the L2. Instead, they are encouraged to discover the rules on their own by performing an interactive task with input.

The example below demonstrates a consciousness-raising task concentrating on the indefinite article.

[Consciousness-raising Task Example]

Student 1

1. Correct: There is an apple on the table.

1. Incorrect: There is a apple on the table.

2. Correct: An elephant is crossing the street.

2. Incorrect: A elephant is crossing the street.

3. Correct: A boy is playing baseball.

3. Incorrect: An boy is playing baseball.

Student 2

4. Correct: There is a tree in our yard.

4. Incorrect: There is an tree in our yard.

5. Correct: An ostrich escaped from the zoo.

5. Incorrect: A ostrich escaped from the zoo.

6. Correct: My sister made a birthday cake.

6. Incorrect: My sister made an birthday cake.

(adapted from Wong, 2005, p. 81)

In this task, students are paired and given a set of sentences containing the target form, some of which are grammatically correct while others are not, clearly indicated on the handout. Working together, students read and discuss the sentences, comparing the correct and incorrect ones. Through this process, they determine when and how the target form should be used based on the patterns observed in the sentences. The objective of the task is for students to articulate the rule governing the usage of the target form.

A consciousness-raising task is most effective when dealing with a linguistic form that can be directly compared and has a clear rule. Properly utilized, these tasks assist learners in focusing on grammatical structures they might otherwise overlook. This technique is particularly advantageous when explicit understanding of a grammatical form is desired. It is important to note that in such tasks, learners are presented with both positive evidence (what is grammatical in the L2) and negative evidence (what is ungrammatical in the L2). Moreover, because learners figure out the rules themselves, they tend to retain them better, and the process of self-discovery may encourage them to continue recognizing the target forms autonomously.

Things to Consider 6.1

1. Can you think of cons and pros of each of the input-based techniques?
2. Which of the input-based techniques do you prefer? And why?

Up to this point, we have explored various input-based focus-on-form techniques that teachers can readily incorporate into their classrooms. It is worth noting that all these techniques are proactive because the teacher chooses the target form(s) beforehand. Additionally, it is important to recognize that certain input-based methods like input flood and input enhancement might be too subtle to effectively capture learners' attention to the specific grammatical features being targeted. In such instances, combining implicit techniques with more explicit focus-on-form techniques, such as output-based techniques discussed in the following section, could be beneficial.

Output-Based Techniques

Things to Consider 6.2

1. To what extent did producing language output contribute to your personal efforts in learning a second language?
2. Drawing from your own experience, what significance does output hold in the process of acquiring a second

language?

As discussed in Chapter 4, the importance of output in L2 learning was initially underscored by Swain (1985) in her Output Hypothesis. Ever since then, the facilitative role of output in L2 learning has been proved both theoretically and experimentally. The role output plays in learning L2 suggested in SLA research can be listed as follows (Nassaji & Fotos, 2011).

1. Leaners have an opportunity for syntactic processing. When learners listen or read, they simply need to grasp the gist of the message, but when they speak or write, they also need to pay close attention to how the meaning is expressed and encoded.
2. Learners have a chance to modify their initial output to make it more comprehensible to the interlocutor while negotiating for meaning.
3. Learners realize that they are not able to express their thoughts as they intend (noticing the hole), or they recognize discrepancies between their utterances and those of native speakers (interlocutors) (noticing the gap). Consequently, their output prompts them to notice their linguistic shortcomings and raises their awareness of what they need to focus on learning the L2.
4. Learners have an opportunity to test their hypotheses (e.g., whether they can use certain linguistic forms or not). Successful communication serves as confirmation of these hypotheses. Conversely, in instances of communication

breakdown, learners observe their interlocutor's response, obtaining valuable feedback. Armed with this feedback, they can adjust their language output to enhance its comprehensibility for the interlocutors.

5. Learners can be encouraged to consciously reflect on language as they consider what to express and how to articulate it (i.e., metalinguistic function). This reflective process in using language aids learners in gaining control over their language use and internalizing their linguistic knowledge.
6. Learners receive input that is more precisely tailored to their proficiency levels while they are negotiating for meaning.
7. Learners develop automaticity of their existing knowledge as output provides them with ample opportunities to practice L2.

Next, let's consider two output-focused techniques commonly employed in second language research and educational settings: dictogloss and text reconstruction. These activities are designed to prompt learners to actively produce language output and participate in thoughtful reflection and discussion regarding their language use with peers.

Dictogloss

In dictogloss (also referred as dicto-comp), students recreate a text or story that the teacher reads to them: the teacher reads a paragraph at normal speed, typically repeating it two or three times, and then asks the students to rewrite the paragraph based on what they remember. Afterward, the students compare their recreated version of the text with the teacher's original one. This process directs the students' focus towards particular language forms. This activity can be done individually or in pairs (i.e., collaborative writing).

In order to employ dictogloss effectively, it is important to choose a text that suits the level of the learners (e.g., beginners - 3 to 4 sentences; intermediate - 6 to 8 sentences; advanced - 8 to 12 sentences). It has four stages:

Stage 1: Preparation
The teacher introduces the topic, if necessary, the language focus and the key vocabulary.

Stage 2: Dictation
The teacher reads the text at a slightly slower speed than native speaker speed. Read the text again at native speaker speed and, on the second reading, students individually make very brief notes (sentence fragments) on main ideas. Remember that the purpose is to get the main ideas, not every word exactly as it appears in the text, so do not read too slowly.

Stage 3: Reconstruction
Students reconstruct the passage in pairs by comparing notes and write a shared version of the text, editing for accurate punctuation, spelling and inclusion of the main

ideas.

Stage 4: Analysis and correction

Students compare reconstructions with other groups and with the original. Discuss the differences.

In Stage 2, students are primarily focused on understanding the passage, involving themselves in semantic processing. Moving on to Stage 3, students review their notes and reconstruct the text using their own language, aiming for making it as close to the original as. In this phase, students are involved in syntactic processing, wherein they build sentences by incorporating grammar and function words alongside the content words they have jotted down. It is important to note that, at this point, learners are pushed to undertake syntactic processing. During Stage 4, students are able to notice the gap between their text and the teacher's original version, which may enable them to raise their awareness of the language forms. Consider the example below which aims to teach the use of relative clauses:

[Dictogloss Activity Example 1]

Friendship

We are always looking for good friends. These days it is hard to find true friends whom we can trust. Certainly, it is important to be considerate of those who care for us. However, a true friend is someone who is sincere and loyal, and is with us through tough times. We don't have to wonder if a friend, who is busy with a new partner and three kids, will have time to comfort us after a bad day. However, a true friendship is like a bridge that is built with planks of loyalty. It is that kind of connection that binds us together.

Procedure for completing the task:

1. Preparation and warm-up: discuss the importance of friendship and the different ways in which someone can be a friend. Examine the different characteristics of a good friend. Also, tell the class that they are going to hear a text on friendship. Ask them what they guess the text would include. Explain difficult vocabulary (e.g., trust, loyalty, and considerate).
2. Dictation: read the text at a normal pace. Ask students to jot down the words related to the content as you read.
3. Reconstruction: ask learners to form groups of two or three and pool their resources to reconstruct the text as closely as possible to the original.
4. Analysis and correction: when they finish, ask learners to analyze and compare their original versions. Go around the class and help learners to correct their errors.

Using a dictogloss has several advantages (Nassaji & Fotos, 2011). First, it integrates the four language skills of listening, reading, speaking, and writing. Second it requires learners to participate in discussions concerning suitable lexical and grammatical forms, pushing them to reflect on their own L2 output and engaging them in talking about language itself. Third, it caters to both individuals and groups. Fourth, it encourages learners to pool their knowledge and learn from each other. Finally, it achieves balance between memory (where learners recollect the text's content from memory) and creativity (where learners employ their individual linguistic abilities during the reconstruction process).

The text employed for a dictogloss task can either be an authentic text or something generated or adjusted by the teacher to suit their students. It would be beneficial if the text includes multiple instances of a specific grammatical form, helping to focus learners' attention on the target structures within the text. Dictogloss is applicable across all levels of L2 proficiency, with simple and brief texts suitable for beginner classes and longer, more linguistically sophisticated texts suitable for advanced classes. Regardless of the proficiency level, careful consideration of the content and complexity of the text is essential. A text that is excessively long and challenging might impose a significant cognitive load on learners, preventing them from completing the task successfully. On the other hand, a text that is too simplistic may not encourage learners to generate output that extends beyond their current interlanguage (Nassaji & Fotos, 2011).

Text Reconstruction

An alternative approach involves a text reconstruction task, wherein students are given a written text. This technique offers flexibility in its application, and the following outlines one simple way in which teachers can integrate it into the classroom.

Steps

1. Select a short-written text suitable for students.
2. Distribute the text to students and have them read the text. Make sure that they understand the text by having them complete some type of comprehension tasks.
3. Collect the text from the students.
4. Ask them to get into groups of three or four.
5. Distribute another version of the text to each group. In this version, the initial text is altered so that all functional words are eliminated, leaving only the content words.
6. Make students collaborate to reconstruct the text by inserting suitable function words, inflectional morphemes, cohesive devices, and other elements, aiming to produce a meaningful, coherent, and grammatically accurate passage.
7. Provide each group with the original text and instruct students to compare their written work with the original passage.

Things to Consider 6.3

1. What are some of the similarities and differences between a dictogloss and a text reconstruction task?
2. Which one could be easier for students and why?

Dictogloss and text reconstruction share a commonality in providing students with chances to contemplate their language usage while engaging in collaborative writing discussions with their peers.

Researchers are intrigued by the interactions among learners during this process because it is valuable for examining whether and how learners reflect on language, thus illustrating the reflective/metalinguistic function of output. This interaction is called language-related episodes (LREs). Typical LREs involve learners questioning their language use, deliberating about language choices, and giving and receiving feedback. Some LREs that emerged from a dictogloss task using the text below are shown in Sample LRE 1 and 2:

> [Dictogloss Text]
> Once, in a pretty village surrounded by hills and fields, there was a girl named Emily. Emily always wanted to see places far from her small town. She liked to learn about different countries and their cultures. Emily never went far away before, but now she saved enough money for her first trip alone. She spent a long time getting ready for this big trip.
>
> [Sample LRE #1]
> S1: ...surround.... surround by, right?
> S2: I think surrounded ... it's surrounded by...
> S1: Oh...yeah, this is good, right?
> S3: Surrounded by hill. Yes, this is better.....
>
> [Sample LRE #2]
> S1: get ready or getting ready... Which one is correct?
> S2: getting ready? I don't know.
> S3: Hmm... getting ready for... I heard getting...

S1: Okay, getting ready...

We have explored the various functions of output and discussed a couple of output-based techniques. The presented techniques force learners' written output and promote collaborative efforts. Collaborative writing tasks prove to be an effective means of allowing learners to combine their linguistic capabilities and engage in thoughtful discussions about their language use, both their own and that of their peers, as they strive to convey meaning. It is crucial not to underestimate the role of output in second language (L2) learning, as it is through the production of output that learners become aware of gaps and deficiencies in their interlanguage. This awareness, in turn, motivates them to seek relevant L2 data to address and fill these gaps and holes.

Interaction-based Techniques: Interactional Corrective Feedback

The role of interaction in L2 learning has widely discussed and explored ever since Long (1996) proposed the Interaction Hypothesis. As discussed in Chapter 4, it has been claimed that negotiation for meaning during interaction facilitates L2 acquisition "because it connects input, internal learner capacities, particularly selective attention, and output in productive ways" (Long, 1996, pp. 451–452). Interaction holds significance as various types of modifications take place during negotiated exchanges. These adjustments push the learner to make his output more comprehensible to the interlocutor (modified output) and enable the learner to receive interactional corrective feedback on his inaccurate and inappropriate utterances. This interactional corrective feedback, embedded within meaning-focused exchanges, ensures that attention to linguistic form takes place precisely when the learner is processing meaning (Mackey, 1999, 2006, 2012; Nassaji, 2020). This, in turn, offers learners opportunities to establish connections between linguistic form and meaning, essential for second language development.

Types of Interactional Corrective Feedback

Interactional corrective feedback can occur in a variety of ways. A distinction lies in the categorization of feedback into input-providing and output-prompting types, determined by whether the teacher provides the correct form to learners or attempts to elicit it from them (Lyster & Ranta, 1997; Lyster & Saito, 2010).

A common type of input-providing feedback is a recast, which maintains the general meaning of an utterance while correcting the linguistic error (Nicholas et al., 2001). Consider the following example.

Recasts

Student: when I was soldier, I used to wear the balaclava

Teacher: and why did you wear it Will, for protection from the cold or for another reason

Will: just wind uh protection to wind and cold

Teacher: protection from

Will: uh from wind and cold

Teacher: right, okay not for a disguise

In this example, Will and the teacher are having a conversation about his military experiences. When Will makes a preposition error, the teacher provides the accurate form in a recast. Following Will's repetition of the correct form, the conversation proceeds to further discussions about his experiences.

As the example shows, when providing a recast, the teacher promptly gives the accurate form immediately after Will commits an error. This action could lead to the situation where Will becomes aware of the gap between his initial utterance and the correct form (noticing the gap). Put differently, the juxtaposition of an accurate form with an erroneous one aids Will in recognizing the gap (Long, 1996, 2007). Furthermore, recasts are generally implicit and do not interrupt the flow of communication (Long, 2007). In spite of these advantages, recasts frequently face criticisms for being overly implicit, making it challenging for learners to recognize them as corrective feedback, especially when they engage in meaning-based communication. Depending on the delivery of recasts, learners might interpret them as confirmations of their original statements rather than as corrections (Kim & Han, 2007; Lyster 1998, Mackey et al., 2000).

Another form of input-providing feedback is explicit correction. Let's consider the following example and observe the differences from recasts (Loewen, 2015).

Explicit Correction

Student: when I was soldier, I used to wear the balaclava

Teacher: and why did you wear it Will, for protection from the cold or for another reason

Will: just wind uh protection to wind and cold

Teacher: not protection to... protection from

Will: uh from wind and cold

Teacher: right, okay not for a disguise

In this example, the teacher provides the correct form with a direct indication, highlighting that Will has made an error in contrast to recasts.

In contrast to input-providing feedback, output-prompting feedback does not provide learners with the correct form. Instead, it encourages the learner, either explicitly or implicitly, to repair their ill-formed or inappropriate utterances (i.e., self-correction). Output-prompting feedback also referred to as "prompts" because it prompts learners to generate modified output. This category encompasses elicitation including clarification requests, metalinguistic feedback, and repetitions.

Clarification Requests

Student: I got home about eight and I go swimming.

Teacher: Huh?

Student: I went to swimming with my friends.

Clarification requests may be implicit as seen in the example above, or if the teacher responds with something like *What*? or *Can you say that again*? Alternatively, other elicitations, such as *Can you say that again correctly*? are more explicit. Employing such elicitation techniques offers the advantage of prompting learners to engage in deeper cognitive processing, requiring self-correction or modified output (Li, 2010), which is argued to enhance second language (L2) learning. However, learners need a certain level of explicit knowledge about the linguistic form being targeted. In other words, learners must possess relevant explicit knowledge about the target form, which might not be proceduralized enough to use in spontaneous communication. Without this knowledge, they may struggle to self-correct the targeted structure.

Metalinguistic Feedback

Student: Peter… he… was with friend and drink… beer a lot.

Teacher: drink? You're talking about what Peter did yesterday.

Student: Oh, yes… Peter drank with friends.

Metalinguistic feedback conveys information about the nature of an error in a more direct and disruptive manner. This explicit feedback can significantly divert learners' attention from meaning-focused interactions, as they become more focused on the linguistic structures. Nevertheless, the overt identification of errors in metalinguistic feedback increases the likelihood of learners noticing both the feedback and the structures being targeted. For instance, the example above, extracted from a task where learners described a character's activities from the previous day, leaves no doubt as to the nature of the error.

Things to Consider 6.4

1. Based on your learning experiences, which type of interactional corrective feedback do you prefer and why?
2. Can you identify some factors that teachers should consider when employing interactional corrective

feedback?

Among interactional corrective feedback types, L2 research has found that recasts are the most frequently used in the meaning-based classroom. As noted previously, this might be due to the fact that recasts tend to be implicit and nondisruptive, thus not interrupting the flow of communication. In addition, recasts offer not only positive evidence (correct form) but also negative evidence (a signal of the occurrence of the error). However, ironically, these benefits could render recasts ineffective in cases where learners do not recognize them as corrections, as illustrated in the following example.

Student: How many people you will invite?
Teacher: How many people will I invite?
Student: Yes, many people? I want to go.

(Kim & Han, 2007)

In this example, the learner interprets recasts as a confirmation check, leading her to continue expressing her intended message. Indeed, a considerable amount of research has highlighted this issue. However, it should not be interpreted that recasts need to be avoided.

Things to Consider 6.5

Let's compare the following example to the one above from Kim and Han (2007). And, consider which one seems more explicit than the other and why.

Student: Everyone don't want to pay.

Teacher: Everyone **doesn't** want to pay. (stress on doesn't)

Student: Doesn't want to.

Several factors can influence the level of explicitness in recasts, including how they are given, the specific language aspects targeted (such as morphosyntax, phonology, and vocabulary), and the learner's focus on accuracy. Studies have shown that learners who prioritize accuracy are more inclined to recognize recasts as corrections compared to those who prioritize fluency (Mackey & Goo, 2007). It falls upon the teacher to determine the most effective types of corrective feedback based on the learning environment and the tendencies of the learners (Li, 2010, 2013).

Chapter Summary

There is substantial evidence supporting the integration of focus on form within second language (L2) classrooms. Learners can benefit from attending to language features while participating in communicative tasks. While some learners may naturally notice language forms, often, it is necessary for teachers to draw learners' attention towards the target forms. There are a variety of techniques teachers can use for this, ranging from implicit approaches like input flood and input enhancement to slightly more explicit strategies such as corrective feedback. While focus on form can prove effective, it does not render explicit instruction unnecessary. There are situations where a more direct and explicit approach may be necessary. In other word, focusing on form is one approach in L2 instruction, and the teaching methods should be adaptable based on learners' individual differences (see Chapter 8).

Chapter 7

Sociocultural Approach and Instructed SLA

1. Key Concepts of Sociocultural Theory

2. Cooperative Language Learning

3. Chapter Summary

Chapter 7

Sociocultural Approach and Instructed SLA

Things to Consider 7.1

Read the following statement related to sociocultural theory and answer the questions.

According to the sociocultural perspective, our psychological development is influenced by mentors like teachers and parents, as well as by our involvement in social circles and cultural activities.

1. Based on your understanding of the explanation above, can you guess key words that would characterize the sociocultural theory?
2. Do you agree with the statement provided? If so, why? If not, why not?

Second language learning theories based on cognitive approaches

perceive second language interaction as a source of input processed by internal learning mechanisms. However, an alternative perspective, known as sociocultural theory, contends that interaction forms the basis of the learning process, emphasizing its social rather than individual nature. This theory draws inspiration from Lev Vygotsky (1978, 1986, 1987), a prominent figure in early Soviet psychology, whose research primarily focused on children's first language development. Vygotsky's insights into language acquisition among children have been developed by second language researchers to explain second language learning. To understand Vygotsky's views on language development, Lantolf (2000) suggests that one needs to understand the concept of mediation:

> The central and distinguishing concept of sociocultural theory is that higher forms of human mental activity are mediated. Vygotsky (1987) argued that just as humans do not act directly on the physical world but rely, instead, on tools and labor activity, we also use symbolic tools, or signs, to mediate and regulate our relationships with others and with ourselves... Included among symbolic tools are numbers and arithmetic systems, music, art, and above all, language. As with physical tools, humans use symbolic artifacts to establish an indirect, or mediated, relationship between ourselves and the world.
>
> (Lantolf, 2000, p. 80)

Sociocultural perspectives claim that learning occurs through mediated tools, with language serving as a central tool for cognition ('tool for thought'). Additionally, learning is perceived as socially mediated, primarily through face-to-face interaction. It occurs as individuals collaboratively tackle problems alongside experts as well as peers.

Key Concepts of Sociocultural Theory

ZDP and Scaffolding

Vygotsky's theory introduces two key concepts: the Zone of Proximal Development (ZPD) and scaffolding. The ZPD is defined as "the difference between the child's actual developmental level, as determined by independent problem-solving, and the higher level of potential development, as determined through problem-solving under adult guidance or collaboration with more capable peers" (Vygotsky, 1978, p. 85). In simpler terms, it represents the space between a child's current developmental stage and the stage they can achieve with assistance from others. Vygotsky emphasizes that instruction is effective only when it "marches ahead of development and leads it" (Vygotsky, 1986, p. 188).

The Zone of Proximal Development (ZPD) has been adapted within the field of second language acquisition, with the concept of assistance often referred to as *scaffolding*. Some interpretations of scaffolding align closely with Vygotsky's original notion of ZPD, emphasizing social mediation involving interaction between individuals, typically an expert and a learner. However, in the context of second language learning, scaffolding encompasses various forms, including learner consultation of resources like grammar books or dictionaries, as well as teacher corrective feedback. Although the scope of scaffolding could vary, the basic principle of sociocultural theory is that second language learners progress to higher levels of linguistic proficiency through collaboration and interaction with individuals who possess greater proficiency in the second language.

Other Regulation and Self-Regulation

In sociocultural theory, successful learning involves a transition from collaborative engagement with others (inter-mental activity) to independent internal processes (intra-mental activity). Initially, individuals rely on external guidance from more skilled peers in what is termed other-regulation. As they absorb new skills and knowledge, they become self-regulated, capable of autonomous action and self-management. This transformation is facilitated through scaffolding, particularly within the Zone of Proximal Development (ZPD). A notable aspect of self-regulated individuals is the use of private speech, or inner speech, which signifies their ability to regulate their own behavior. Private speech, an evolution from social language interactions, serves as a tool for thought in fully autonomous learners. Learners are viewed as active creators of their learning environments.

Collective Scaffolding and Cooperation

As previously mentioned, sociocultural theory initially posits that development evolves through interaction with a more knowledgeable interlocutor. However, some scholars have expanded the concept of scaffolding to encompass support from peers of similar proficiency level (Ohta, 2001; Swain & Lapkin, 1998, 2002). Although learners may be considered to have the similar L2 proficiency based on a certain type of test, they may in fact have different L2 knowledge and expertise. The process of pooling each other's knowledge, which is referred by collective scaffolding (Donato, 1994), leads learners to co-construct new knowledge and consequently solve language problems they encounter during a task (Storch, 2002, 2005). The dialogue used during this process is called the Language Related Episodes (LREs) or meta-talk (i.e., an instance where learners deliberate about their use of language). The LREs show the process of collective scaffolding as in the examples below, which contains two consecutive LREs. The first LRE is a lexical one, and the second is a form-based LRE.

[Lexical and Form-Based LREs]

Mat: By forcing the students to revising
Emily: Encouraging would be a nicer word
Mat: Ha ha ha. In the encouraging the students [lexical LRE]
Emily: To take the initiative
Mat: Yeah, great.
Emily: To take initiative to start revising... to start a revision. Oh no, to start revising, no?
Mat: mmm... to start revising. [form-based LRE]

(Wigglesworth & Storch, 2009, p. 459)

García Mayo's (2002) examples of the LREs below also illustrate how two learners engage in collaborative interaction to arrive at the correct linguistic form.

[Example 1]

Student 1: After running up the stairs I was quite... breath... out of breath?...

Student 2: Out of breath?

Student 1: I think it is out of breath because without breath sound weird, and...

Student 2: Yeah, out of breath sounds better

[Example 2]

Student 1: ... mean are less incline... it has to be an adjective... inclined to confess, you are inclined to do something

Student 2: To confession

Student 1: To confess...To confess what?

Student 2: But after a preposition... to is a preposition

Student 1: Yeah

Student 2: So it should be followed by ing...

Student 1: Inclined to confessing...

Student 2: Yeah...

Student 1: No, because to is part of the second verb... inclined to confess... yeah

Student 2: Ok, I trust you

(García Mayo, 2002, p. 329)

As learners produce the Language Related Episode (LRE), they question their language use, or correct themselves or others (Swain & Lapkin, 1995). It has been reported that the quality and quantity of the LREs have contributed to L2 learning.

Cooperative Language Learning

Things to Consider 7.2

1. Have you ever worked on a task or project with others? Did you find your experience pleasant or not?
2. Can you explain why your experience of working with others pleasant or unpleasant?

As previously mentioned, Vygotsky's theory underlines the importance of the zone of proximal development and scaffolding. Scaffolding naturally fosters collaborative dialogue (Swain, 2000), which is a type of discourse where new knowledge or skills emerge through interaction. Cooperative language learning (CLL) is closely linked to these ideas, offering learners chances to engage in collaborative dialogues.

CLL aligns with sociocultural learning theory by aiming to establish an environment that encourages mutual assistance (Alghamdi & Gillies, 2013). Newman and Holtzman (1993) highlights that Vygotsky's approach emphasized cooperation by forming diverse groups of children and assigning tasks that required collaborative effort, thus fostering joint activity and cooperation among them. In addition to sociocultural theory, the interactional approach (refer to Chapter 4) is also pertinent to CLL because CLL activities create an ideal setting for negotiation of meaning.

Cooperative learning was promoted and developed in the US in the 1960s and 1970s. Before discussing the application of CLL in second language teaching, it is important to first define cooperative learning in general:

> Cooperative learning is group learning activity organized so that learning is dependent on the socially structured exchange of information between learners in groups and in which each learner is held accountable for his or her own learning and is motivated to increase the learning of others.
>
> (Olsen & Kagan, 1992, p. 8)

CLL in Second Language Instruction

In second language teaching, CLL is perceived as a learner-centered approach to teaching, which is believed to provide benefits over traditional teacher-fronted classroom methods. In language teaching, its objectives are:

1. To provide opportunities for naturalistic second langue acquisition through the use of interactive pair and group activities;
2. To provide teachers with a methodology to enable them to achieve this goal and one that can be applied in a variety of

curriculum settings (e.g., content-based, foreign language classrooms, mainstreaming);

3. To enable focused attention to particular lexical items, language structures, and communicative functions through the use of interactive tasks;
4. To provide opportunities for learners to develop successful learning and communication strategies;
5. To enhance learner motivation and reduce learner stress and to create a positive affective classroom climate.

(Adapted from Richard & Rodgers, 2014, p. 245)

The term 'cooperative' in Cooperative Language Learning emphasizes another significant feature of CLL: its focus on creating classrooms that cultivate cooperation instead of competition in the learning process (Kagan & Kagan, 1994; McCafferty, 2006). Advocates of CLL highlight the advantages of cooperation in enhancing learning:

> Cooperation is working together to accomplish shared goals. Within cooperative situations, individuals seek outcomes beneficial to themselves and all other group members. Cooperative learning is the instructional use of small groups through which students work together to maximize their own and each other's learning. It may be contrasted with competitive learning in which students work against each other to achieve an academic goal such as a grade of "A."
>
> (Johnson et al., 1994, p. 4)

From the perspective of second language teaching, McGroarty (1989) identifies several learning advantages for ESL students in CLL classrooms:

1. ESL students in CLL classrooms benefit from more frequent and diverse opportunities to practice their second language through various forms of interaction.
2. They have the chance to develop or use language skills in manners that aid cognitive growth and enhance linguistic abilities.
3. Integration of language with Content-Based Instruction becomes feasible.
4. A wider array of educational materials can be incorporated to support both language and conceptual learning.
5. Students are provided with chances to serve as mutual resources for one another, thereby taking on more active roles in their learning process.

When applying CLL in the classroom, the effectiveness of the approach heavily relies on the type and arrangement of group work. It requires a well-structured learning program carefully created to facilitate learner interaction and motivation to enhance each other's learning. Olsen and Kagan (1992) propose the following essential components for successful group-based learning in CLL:

Positive Interdependence

Positive interdependence is a central aspect of cooperative and collaborative learning, where individuals within a group with shared objectives recognize that collaborating is advantageous both individually and collectively. Success is contingent upon the active participation of all members. Positive interdependence, which fosters cooperation, leads to promotive interaction where individuals support and assist their teammates in accomplishing tasks. Conversely, negative interdependence, rooted in competition, prompts interactions where team members strive to impede the success of others on their team while advancing their individual objectives. Simply engaging in interpersonal interactions does not inherently enhance productivity or elevate achievement in learning groups; rather, positive interdependence is essential for yielding such outcomes.

Individual Accountability

Individual accountability in cooperative learning refers to the expectation that every member of a collaborative group is responsible for their own learning and contributions to the group task. It implies that each student is accountable for their participation, effort, and understanding of the material under study. Individual accountability ensures that each student's efforts are recognized and valued within the group, promoting a sense of responsibility and commitment to the collective success of the team. This concept helps prevent free-riding or passive participation within cooperative learning settings and encourages active engagement and involvement from all group members.

There are numerous ways to structure and enhance individual accountability within cooperative learning environments. These include maintaining small group sizes, administering individual tests, or conducting random oral examinations to assess understanding. When students are required to present information in front of their peers, teachers can ensure individual accountability by closely monitoring group dynamics and individual contributions. Individual accountability can be structured by assigning one student in each group to check for understanding. The checker poses questions, and the other group members provide rational answers supporting group answers. Additionally, students can enhance their understanding by teaching others or reviewing and improving each other's work (Johnson, Johnson, & Holubec, 1998).

Social Skills

Social skills encompass the behaviors we employ to articulate ideas, emotions, viewpoints, affection, as well as to sustain or enhance our relationships with others, and to address and fortify social situations (Mahinpo, 2012). Within cooperative learning groups, students not only acquire academic knowledge and skills related to their tasks but also develop interpersonal and small group abilities (teamwork). Consequently, groups must possess the capacity for effective leadership, decision-making, trust-building, communication, and conflict resolution. Considering the complicated nature of these skills, teachers can significantly enhance student performance by integrating cooperative skill components into their cooperative lessons.

Structuring and Structures

Structuring and structures refer to ways to organizing student interaction and different ways in which student are to interact in a classroom (Kagan, 1989). Sequential methods are employed to introduce, practice, and review material. Certain techniques facilitate communication between pairs, while others are best for teamwork, and some involve the entire class. Here are some examples of cooperative structuring:

1. Three-step interview. (1) Students pair up, taking turns as the interviewer and interviewee. (2) They switch roles afterward. (3) Each student then shares what they learned from both interviews with their partner.
2. Roundtable. There is one sheet of paper and one pen assigned to each team. (1) A student contributes and (2) passes the paper and pen to the student on their left. (3) Each student takes turns contributing. When conducted verbally, this structure is referred to as Round Robin.
3. Think-Pair-Share. (1) The teacher asks a question, typically one with low consensus. (2) Students individually contemplate a response. (3) They then engage in discussions with a partner about their responses. (4) Finally, students present their partner's responses to the class.
4. Solve-Pair-Share. (1) The teacher presents a problem, which could be a low-consensus or high-consensus item, often solvable through various strategies. (2) Students independently work on finding solutions. (3) They then describe their problem-solving approaches using Interview or Round Robin formats.

(Adapted from Richard & Rodgers, 2014, pp. 251-252)

Chapter Summary

The sociocultural perspective highlights the importance of learning through interaction with individuals who are more knowledgeable and can offer guidance, a concept known as scaffolding. However, L2 research indicates that learners also benefit from interaction with peers, reinforcing the educational notion that "No one knows nothing. Everyone has a piece of the puzzle." In this sense, cooperative language learning emerges as a fitting approach for L2 classrooms, though its implementation demands substantial preparation and learners' understanding of the advantages of collaboration. Establishing a cooperative learning environment requires significant time and effort; nevertheless, considering the potential benefits, the endeavor proves worthwhile (Dörnyei,1997; Shaaban & Ghaith, 2005).

Chapter 8

Individual Differences and Instructed SLA

1. Motivation
2. Personality
3. Languag Learning Aptitude
4. Learning Styles
5. Learning Strategies
6. Age

Chapter 8

Individual Differences and Instructed SLA

Things to Consider 8.1

1. Do you think you are good at learning a second language? Why or why not?
2. Which elements do you believe influence the outcome of second language acquisition?

A well-established observation regarding second language acquisition is the considerable variation among learners in both the pace and level of proficiency achieved. These Individual differences have been characterized as psychological traits that remain relatively consistent within an individual but vary across different learners. Numerous studies have explored how these individual traits correlate with success in language learning (Dörnyei, 2005). This correlation is typically explored by assessing learners' characters through questionnaires and evaluating their language proficiency through language tests.

Individua differences have been categorized in different ways within second language acquisition research, as illustrated in Table 8.1. Within this spectrum, this chapter discusses several significant factors influencing individual differences in second language acquisition. These factors include motivation, aptitude, personality, learning styles, learning strategies, and the age at which learning begins.

Table 8.1 Taxonomies of Individual Differences in Second Language Teaching

Robinson (2002)	Dörnyei (2005)	Ellis (2008)
Intelligence	Personality	Intelligence
Motivation	Language aptitude	Working memory
Anxiety	Motivation	Language aptitude
Learning aptitude	Learning and cognitive styles	Learning styles
Working memory	Language learning strategies	Motivation
Age	Other learner characteristics (e.g., anxiety, self-esteem, learner beliefs, creativity, and willingness to communicate)	Anxiety
		Personality
		Willingness to communicate
		Learner beliefs
		Learning strategies

(Adapted from Ellis, 2008)

Regarding instructed second language acquisition, it can be helpful to differentiate between individual differences that can be modified and those that remain relatively stable. According to Dörnyei (2005), while individual differences tend to persist within individuals, some are more susceptible to change, such as motivation, beliefs, and learning strategies. These traits have more potential for adjustment within the classroom environment. Conversely, other individual differences like aptitude and personality are relatively fixed (Dörnyei & Skehan, 2003). Consequently, the implication for instructed second language acquisition is for teachers and learners to recognize and understand these influences in the classroom rather than attempting to alter them.

Motivation

Motivation is often acknowledged by both teachers and learners as a primary factor influencing second language (L2) acquisition in the classroom (Dörnyei, 2005). However, not all scholars posit a direct causal relationship between motivation and the individual differences observed in L2 learning (e.g., Sparks et al., 2023). Nevertheless, many researchers and teachers are concerned with how to increase learner motivation in the classroom. Extensive research has consistently demonstrated that motivation strongly correlates with success in language acquisition (Dörnyei, 2001a, 2001b). In other words, motivation is the driving force pushing learners to initiate and sustain their engagement in their L2 learning process (Dörnyei, 2005).

Gardner's Model

Robert Gardner stands out as a significant figure in the field of motivation within second language acquisition. Gardner (1985) posits that for a student to be deemed motivated, four elements must be present: a goal, a desire to achieve such goal, positive attitudes, and exerted effort.

Gardner's framework is fundamentally centered around integration, which represents an individual's tendency towards the target language community and their inclination to interact or identify with it. Masgoret and Gardner (2003) highlights integrativeness as a factor that fuels an individual's motivation to learn a second language, where motivation is essential for actual achievement in the language (referred to as integrative motivation). Furthermore, instrumental orientation (referred to as instrumental motivation), which generally pertains to learners' practical reasons for studying a language such as employment prospects or academic requirements, also contributes to language proficiency. Gardner places greater emphasis on integrative motivation over instrumental motivation.

Gardner's socio-educational model has significantly shaped research on the correlation between motivation and second language acquisition. Nonetheless, doubts have been raised regarding its applicability, particularly since the model was initially constructed within bilingual contexts in Canada, where integration into the second language culture is crucial. Moreover, in the case of English becoming a lingua franca, the integrative aspect might be somewhat diminished (Loewen, 2015).

Another criticism surrounding the socio-educational model is that it sees motivation as a fairly stable and consistent characteristic. However, starting from the 1990s, motivation research has shifted towards a process-oriented perspective. In this perspective, motivation is seen as dynamic and subject to change.

Dörnyei's Model

Dörnyei and his colleagues (e.g., Dörnyei, 2005; Dörnyei & Ottó, 1998) introduce the process-oriented motivation model. This model illustrates how an individual learner's motivation gradually changes over time: the preactional stage, the actional stage, and the postactional stage. The preactional stage, also known as choice motivation, involves the generation of motivation and the selection of a goal to pursue. The actional stage, or executive motivation, concerns the maintenance of the activity. Lastly, the postactional stage, termed motivation retrospection, occurs after the completion of the action and entails reflection on the activity, assessment, and subsequent progress (Dörnyei, 2005). Drawing from this process-oriented model, Dörnyei (2001a) proposed a framework for implementing motivational teaching practices.

1. Creating the basic motivational condition, which involves establishing good social relations and a positive learning atmosphere
2. Generating initial motivation, which involves building students' interest in and positive attitudes to learning the language
3. Maintaining and protecting motivation, comprising pedagogical strategies for keeping students well motivated and involved during the learning process
4. Encouraging positive retrospective self-evaluation, which entails enhancing students' self-perceptions of competence and success

Based on prior motivation research, Dörnyei (2005) introduces the Second Language (L2) Motivational Self System, comprising the ideal L2 self, the ought-to L2 self, and L2 learning experiences. The ideal L2 self-concept suggests that motivation for L2 acquisition is heightened when learners envision their ideal selves as proficient in a second language. The ought-to L2 self pertains to feelings of obligation regarding L2 learning, such as perceiving it as a necessary endeavor. This dimension of motivation may deviate from learners' personal desires. Second language learning experiences encompass the executive motivation associated with the immediate learning environment and encounters. Dörnyei (2005) also reconceptualizes integrativeness not as a desire to identify with the target language community but as a drive to bridge the gap between the actual self and the ideal L2 self.

Intrinsic and Extrinsic Motivation

Motivation can also be categorized based on whether learners are driven by internal or external factors to achieve success in a task. Edward Deci (1975) provided a definition for intrinsic motivation:

> Intrinsically motivated activities are ones for which there is no apparent reward except the activity itself. People seem to engage in the activities for their own sake and not because they led to an extrinsic reward... Intrinsically motivated behaviors are aimed at brining about certain internally rewarding consequences, namely, feelings of competence and self-determination. (p. 23)

Conversely, extrinsic motivation is driven by the expectation of a reward external to the individual. Common extrinsic rewards include money, prizes, grades, and specific forms of positive feedback.

Things to Consider 8.2

1. Can you recall any activity you've engaged in with intrinsic motivation thus far?
2. Can you recall any activity you've engaged in with extrinsic motivation thus far?
3. Which form of motivation do you think is more powerful?

Differentiating between the intrinsic-extrinsic construct and Gardner's integrative-instrumental orientation is crucial. Although numerous cases of intrinsic motivation may align with integrative orientation, not all do. Bailey (1986) illustrated the relationship between these two dichotomies using the diagram provided in Table 8.2.

Table 8.2. Motivational Dichotomies

	Intrinsic	Extrinsic
Integrative	L2 learner wishes to integrate with the L2 culture (e.g., for immigration or marriage)	Someone else wishes the L2 learner to know the L2 for integrative reasons (e.g., Korean parents send children to Korean language school)
Instrumental	L2 learner wishes to achieve goals utilizing L2 (e.g., for a career)	External power wants L2 learner to learn the L2 (e.g., cooperation sends Korean businessman to U.S. for language training)

(adapted from Brown, 2014)

Motivation and L2 Classrooms

Over time, the understanding of motivation has evolved, but there has been a continuing interest in how to motivate learners in second language classrooms. Researchers have explored various motivational strategies, and Dörnyei and Csizér (1998) proposing the following 10 principles to motivate second language students:

1. Set a personal example with your own behavior.
2. Create a pleasant, relaxed atmosphere in the classroom.
3. Present the tasks properly.
4. Develop a good relationship with the learners.
5. Increase the learners' linguistic self-confidence.
6. Make the language classes interesting.
7. Promote learner autonomy.
8. Personalize the learning process.
9. Increase the learners' goal-orientedness.
10. Familiarize learners with the target language culture.

(Adapted from Dörnyei & Csizér, 1998, p. 215)

Undoubtedly, motivation stands out as a crucial force that drives learners to initiate and sustain their journey in second language acquisition. As mentioned earlier, motivation exhibits a dynamic quality. This implies that learners who exhibit high motivation in the initial stages of language learning may experience a decline in motivation as they progress. It becomes evident that sustaining motivation throughout the learning process is a more challenging task compared to initially sparking learners' interest.

Personality

Personality research has a rich history within psychology. While characterizing one's personality is complex, extroversion/introversion stands out as a commonly used metric for understanding individuals. The stereotype often portrays introverts as finding more joy in solitary activities like reading, whereas extroverts thrive in social settings. These stereotypes carry implications for second language learning success. Some believe that introverts excel academically, supported by empirical findings. But extroverts' sociability suggests they might engage more in language practice, aiding their language development. Thus, it seems that both extroversion and introversion contribute to second language learning success in distinct ways. Extroverts could gain advantages from specific instructional techniques that capitalize on their sociable nature, whereas introverts may achieve success through different approaches tailored to their preferences.

Another aspect frequently discussed in relation to personality is learner anxiety. According to Horwitz, Horwitz, and Cope (1986), anxiety is described as "the subjective feeling of tension, apprehension, nervousness, and worry associated with an arousal of the automatic nervous system" (p. 125). Many second language learners encounter sensations of concern, nervousness, and tension. In initial investigations into learner anxiety, scholars viewed it as a fixed component of one's personality. However, contemporary research suggests that anxiety can be temporary and influenced by the context. Put differently, learners' feelings of unease vary depending on the specific situations they encounter. For example, learners might experience heightened anxiety when delivering oral presentations to the entire class compared to when they engage in group interactions. Anxiety has the potential to disrupt the learning process. However, a certain level of tension can motivate learners to invest additional effort and strive for improved performance, a phenomenon referred to as facilitating anxiety. Other personality traits such as risk-taking, self-esteem, talkativeness, and empathy have been found to be related to L2 achievement to some extent.

It needs to be acknowledged that previous studies on the relationship between personality and L2 outcome have yielded inconclusive findings, which can be attributed to inherent methodological challenges in investigating personality factors. The measurement of personality characteristics poses difficulties, with most studies heavily reliant on individuals' scores from personality questionnaires, which are then correlated with language proficiency tests. For example, questionnaires related to extroversion and introversion may include items such as "Whenever I go somewhere, I develop personal contacts" and "In a large group, I tend to keep silent" (Oxford, 1993). While these questions may to some extent gauge an individual's extroverted or introverted tendencies, responses may vary depending on the specific situation. The interpretation of phrases like "whenever I go somewhere" may be ambiguous, and in the latter question, individuals may tend to speak more about familiar topics than unfamiliar ones. Moreover, the correlation between personality variables and second language learning success may also be influenced by the types of language proficiency tests employed. In other words, the nature of this relationship is likely to vary depending on whether a study employs tests focused on communicative ability or grammatical accuracy.

Despite the mixed findings and inherent challenges in these studies, it is difficult to deny the notion that personality plays a role in the success of second language learning. However, the relationship is complicated, and it is likely that success cannot solely be attributed to personality. Alongside the insights into personality characteristics, other factors such as motivation and additional elements, which will be elaborated upon in this chapter, are also influential contributors to second language learning.

Language Learning Aptitude

Aptitude refers to an individual's inherent capacity for learning new knowledge or mastering skills. When discussing language learning, aptitude specifically pertains to one's strengths in the cognitive processes essential for second language acquisition (Robinson, 2001, 2005). Language aptitude is often regarded as an innate and relatively stable trait that remains unaffected by training (Li, 2013). Furthermore, it is widely recognized as one of the most reliable predictors of success in language learning (Skehan, 1989, 1998).

Things to Consider 8.3

1. Given your understanding of the definition of language learning aptitude, do you believe it correlates with intelligence? Why or why not?
2. What should be tested to evaluate one's language learning ability?

What makes up language aptitude? It includes various elements, with tests designed to assess it incorporating diverse components. However, there are fundamental aspects commonly acknowledged, referred to as the standard four components of language aptitude (Skehan, 1989), which include phonemic coding ability, grammatical sensitivity, inductive learning ability, and memorization ability.

Phonemic coding ability refers to the capability to differentiate sounds in the input and to establish and retain associations between sounds and symbols. This entails not only the skill to discern individual sounds but also to listen to a continuous stream of sound, recognize the phonological boundaries of words, and recall the meaning linked to a specific arrangement of sounds.

Grammatical sensitivity pertains to learners' ability to identify the grammatical roles of words within sentences. It does not focus on learners' understanding of metalinguistic terminology; instead, it emphasizes their ability to discern whether words in various sentences serve similar functions. For instance, the learner is asked to find out which option, among choices (a) through (e) in sentence 2, serves the same role as 'him' in sentence 1.

1. I gave him the book.
2. When Peter's mother died, Mary wrote a letter to him.
(a) (b) (c) (d) (e)

Inductive learning ability is the ability to infer or induce the rules or generalizations about language from samples of the language. In other words, it involves the ability to recognize the grammatical patterns and relationships that are present in the input without being explicitly taught specific grammar rules.

Finally, memorization ability, also known as rote learning ability, focuses on the capacity to create and maintain associations between sounds and meanings. It pertains to learners' capability to memorize and recall second language words and other information.

Skehan (1989) suggests that proficient language learners may not excel in all aspects of aptitude. For instance, some learners may possess strong skills in language analysis but only average memory abilities. This leads to the question of whether practical implications exist for customizing language classrooms based on students' aptitude characteristics. Few studies have delved into this issue, likely due to the challenge of isolating one factor within the complexity of the learning environment that contributes to success or failure. Nonetheless, there have been a handful of relevant studies. For instance, Wesche (1981) and Skehan (1996) found that students exhibited high satisfaction levels when instructional methods aligned with learner characteristics: analytical learners performed better with analytical approaches, while memory-oriented learners did better with methodologies that included exposure to longer chunks of language.

Learning Styles

Things to Consider 8.4

> Picture yourself experiencing the following situation. What actions would you take in this situaction?
>
> I have just arrived at the airport in Komatsu, Japan, around 2:00 a.m. after a stressful day filled with missed flights, delays, and re-routing. The airport is nearly empty, and to make matters worse, my luggage is nowhere to be found. At that late hour, there is nobody who can communicate in English, and my knowledge of Japanese is extremely limited. Additionally, my phone has been stolen.

The manner in which we absorb information and approach challenges appears to be influenced by a somewhat vague connection between personality and cognition, known as cognitive style. When these cognitive styles are specifically associated with an educational setting, particularly where emotions and physiological aspects are intertwined, these cognitive styles are commonly referred to as learning styles.

Learning styles are generally defined as "cognitive, affective, and physiological traits that are relatively stable indicators of how learners perceive, interact with, and respond to the learning environment" (Keefe, 1979, p. 4). Simply put, learning styles is "a general predisposition, voluntary or not, toward processing information in a particular way" (Skehan, 1991, p. 288). A diverse range of learning styles has been identified and studied. From among them, five have been selected due to their significance in teaching contexts. This section will investigate these selected styles.

Field Independence and Dependence

Before exploring field independence, it is important to note that this style stems from an individual's cognitive orientation. Cognitive styles pertain to "consistent individual differences in preferred ways of organizing and processing information and experience" (Messick, 1984, p. 5). These styles ultimately determine how learners engage with learning tasks in second language classrooms, and they are not consciously controlled by learners. Cognitive styles are commonly represented on a value-free bipolar spectrum using continua, and the extremes of these ranges are neither inherently good nor bad. Instead, the extreme of a cognitive style simply denotes a difference rather than a superior or inferior quality.

Field dependence/independence is one of the cognitive styles extensively examined both within and beyond second language acquisition. These cognitive styles pertain to the degree to which an individual favors "an analytic as opposed to a global way of experiencing the environment" (Keefe, 1979, p. 9). Studies on FD/FI have revealed associations between these cognitive styles and various individual traits (Chapelle & Roberts, 1986).

Field dependent (FD) learners perceive their environments holistically, often grasping the overall picture rather than individual components. They typically exhibit extroverted tendencies, are externally driven, and are influenced by peer groups and authority figures. Their empathy and sociability make them inclined to excel in group settings, actively seeking opportunities for interaction with others. These characteristics contribute to their success in acquiring the communicative aspects of language.

On the contrary, field independence (FI) learners approach their surroundings analytically, easily discerning individual pieces of information from the broader context in which they exist. FI learners often exhibit intrinsic motivation and they are driven by self-directed objectives. They also prefer to take charge of their own learning process, seeking solutions independently. They typically have less developed social skills and therefore prefer working alone (Hoffman, 1986, 1997). They are more likely to be good at learning tasks that involve analysis, attention to detail, and mastering exercises.

Left- and Right-Brain Dominance

As a child's brain develops, different functions become specialized in either the left or right hemisphere (i.e., lateralization). The left hemisphere primarily manages speech, abstract thought, and analytical processes, as well as controlling the right side of the body. On the other hand, the right hemisphere handles tasks such as visual processing, spatial reasoning, and controlling movement in the left side of the body. Torrance (1980) outlines various traits associated with dominance of either the left or right brain in Table 8.3.

Table 8.3. Left- and Right-brain Characteristics

Left-Brain Dominance	Right-Brain Dominance
Intellectual	Intuitive
Remembers names	Remembers faces
Responses to verbal instructions and explanations	Responds to demonstrated, illustrated, or symbolic instructions
Experiments systematically and with control	Experiments randomly and with less restraint
Makes objective judgements	Makes subjective judgements
Planned and structured	Fluid and spontaneous
Prefers established, certain information	Prefers elusive, uncertain information
Analytic reader	Synthesizing reader
Reliance on language in thinking and remembering	Reliance on images in thinking and remembering
Favors logical problem solving	Favors intuitive problem solving

(adapted from Torrance, 1980)

Nerve fibers connect the left and right hemispheres of the brain, enabling communication between them in a healthy brain. Essentially, they collaborate and function as a team. Effective problem-solving typically draws upon the capabilities of both hemispheres, and the most successful solutions often emerge when each hemisphere contributes optimally to the process (Danesi, 1988).

However, the left- and right-brain framework provides a valuable lens through which we can explore different learning styles, particularly in the context of second language learning and instruction. Research suggests that individuals with left-brain dominance in second language learning excel in tasks involving the production of isolated words, executing sequential operations, and handling abstract concepts, classification, and reorganization. Conversely, learners with right-brain dominance seem to have strengths in processing holistic images, making generalizations, and expressing emotional responses and artistic creativity (Stevick, 1982).

Things to Consider 8.5

1. Consider the English or other second language classrooms you have experienced. Do you believe learners benefited from the class irrespective of their left- or right-brain dominance? Provide your rationale.
2. Do you think that field independence and dependence correlate with left-brain or right-brain dominance? Why or why not?

Reflectivity and Impulsivity

Psychological research has explored how individuals engage in problem-solving tasks, investigating their tendency to choose for either a rapid and spontaneous (impulsive) response or a slower, more careful (reflective) decision. These two styles are closely associated with the reflective/impulsivity (R/I) continuum (Ewing, 1977): intuitive and systematic styles. Intuitive thinkers rely on gut feelings or hunches, often making multiple attempts before arriving at a solution. Conversely, systematic thinkers thoroughly analyze all aspects of a problem, consider various perspectives, and deliberate extensively before proposing a solution.

The Matching Familiar Figures Test has been employed in the reflectivity/impulsivity research. It requires individuals to identify the item that precisely corresponds to the one displayed at the top of the page, with all items below sharing similarities with the top item. Successfully identifying the matching item demands focused attention. Responses to the task vary, with some individuals taking their time and responding slowly, while others react swiftly. Despite the task's difficulty, some individuals exhibit few errors, whereas others struggle even with straightforward matches. Those who respond quickly and commit numerous errors typically exhibit an impulsive style, whereas individuals who respond slowly and make few errors typically demonstrate a reflective style.

The implications for first language acquisition are numerous. It has been found that children who are conceptually reflective tend to make fewer errors in reading than impulsive children (Kagan, 1965); however, impulsive persons are usually faster readers, and eventually master the 'psycholinguistic guessing game' (Goodman, 1967) of reading so that their impulsive style of reading may not necessarily deter comprehension. It was also reported that inductive reasoning was found to be more effective with reflective persons, suggesting that generally reflective persons could benefit more from inductive learning situations.

Several studies have investigated the relationship between reflective/ impulsive (R/I) tendencies and second language acquisition. Doron (1973) observed that reflective adult learners exhibited slower but more accurate reading abilities compared to impulsive learners. In a separate investigation of adult students, Abraham (1981) suggested a weak correlation between reflection and performance on a proofreading task. Jamieson (1992) discovered that 'fast-accurate' learners, or those who could make good guesses quickly, demonstrated superior language learning abilities as assessed by the standardized Test of English as a Foreign Language. However, she cautioned against assuming that impulsivity always indicates accuracy, as some learners participating in the study were fast yet inaccurate in their responses.

Things to Consider 8.6

1. Which group of learners, impulsive or reflective, would be readily identified as high-performing students in a classroom setting?
2. What are the potential educational applications that can be inferred from the concept of reflective/impulsive tendencies and the outcomes of research studies?

Visual, Auditory, and Kinesthetic Styles

Individual learners exhibit distinct perceptual orientations. Some learners favor reading and studying charts, identifying as visual learners.

These individuals may choose to reorganize lecture notes using color coding or other visual organization methods. Others, known as auditory learners, prefer absorbing information through listening, making lectures an effective mode of learning. Additionally, kinesthetic learners are inclined to express themselves and participate in physical activities that involve bodily movement.

While successful learners may incorporate both visual and auditory input, as well as physical activity, they tend to have a slight preference for one over the other, which can serve as a distinguishing factor among learners. Notably, Reid (1987) discovered significant differences in perceptual orientation based on learners' first language backgrounds; for example, Korean students showed a higher inclination towards visual learning compared to native English speakers, while Japanese students exhibited the least preference for auditory learning.

The discovery that individual learners possess diverse learning styles suggests that teachers could potentially enhance their teaching methods by tailoring them to accommodate the various styles of their students (Dörnyei, 2005; Oxford, 1999). However, implementing personalized instruction poses practical challenges within classroom settings. As an alternative strategy, teachers can diversify their teaching styles. For example, they might incorporate different types of activities where one task involves reading, another involves listening, and yet another involves independent work followed by group collaboration.

Another approach to addressing learning styles involves "style stretching" (Ehrman, 1996), which entails helping learners gain experience operating outside their preferred styles. This can be achieved by first identifying learners' preferred styles through questionnaires designed to raise awareness. Subsequently, learners can engage in activities specifically designed to encourage the use of non-preferred styles. Students can prepare themselves to adapt to various learning environments through 'style stretching.' This training is intricately connected to the cultivation of effective learning strategies, which has gained significance with the growing importance of learner autonomy in achieving success in second language acquisition.

Learner autonomy means the idea that learners should gradually assume greater responsibility for both the content and methods of their learning process. It stems from the belief that students possess the capacity for self-direction and can cultivate an independent, proactive stance towards their academic pursuits. Central to autonomous learning is the student's recognition of their role as an active participant in the learning process. Classroom discussions and one-on-one interactions with the teacher can aid students in comprehending the crucial role they play in achieving success in second language. Students with an autonomous and dynamic approach have the capacity to acquire significantly more knowledge compared to passive and reactive learners. Self-reliant students can proactively address their individual needs, facilitating continuous and meaningful progress. Autonomy entails equipping students with a diverse set of learning strategies that they can skillfully apply across various contexts. Teachers play a crucial role in guiding students to cultivate these learning strategies through learner training within the classroom, and this can take diverse forms and approaches.

Learning Strategies

It is a common observation that certain language learners not only achieve greater success but also employ distinct approaches that set them apart from others. In other words, successful learners often adopt personalized strategies.

Things to Consider 8.7

Rubin and Thompson (1982) provides a summary of fourteen attributes associated with what are commonly referred to as 'good learners.' Take a moment to review these traits and consider how many of them align with your own characteristics.

Good language learners:

a. Find their own way, taking charge of their learning
b. Organize information about language
c. Are creative, developing a 'feel' for the language by experimenting with its grammar and words
d. Make their own opportunities for practice in using the language inside and outside the classroom
e. Learn to live with uncertainty for not getting flustered and by continuing to talk or listen without understanding every word

f. Use mnemonics and other memory strategies to recall what has been learned
g. Make errors work for them and not against them
h. Use linguistics knowledge, including knowledge of their first language in learning a second language
i. Use contextual cues to help them in comprehension
j. Learn to make intelligent guess
k. Learn chunks of language as whole and formalized routines to help them perform 'beyond their competence'
l. Learn certain tricks that help to keep conversations going
m. Learn certain production strategies to fill in gaps in their own competence
n. Learn different styles of speech and writing and learn to vary their language according to the formality of the situation

1. How many of the qualities mentioned above do you see in yourself? Do you believe you qualify as a good language learner based on the characteristics outlined?
2. What common characteristics do good language learners have, according to the list?

Definitions and Types of Learning Strategies

Oxford (2011) defines learning strategies as "the learners' purposeful actions aimed at enhancing language proficiency or achievement, accomplishing a task, or optimizing the efficiency, effectiveness, and ease of learning" (p. 167). For example, when faced with the challenge of memorizing challenging words, learners might consciously opt to associate a new word with one they already know. If this association proves effective in aiding their memory, learners are likely to persist in utilizing this particular strategy.

Oxford (1990) introduces taxonomies of strategy use, categorizing strategies into direct and indirect types. Direct strategies, those assumed to directly impact learning, encompass memory strategies (e.g., forming mental connections, using visual and auditory aids, engaging in physical actions, and reviewing content), cognitive strategies (e.g., practicing, analyzing, taking notes, and summarizing), and compensation strategies (e.g., making educated guesses and overcoming speaking and writing limitations). Indirect strategies, which indirectly support learning, include metacognitive strategies (e.g., organizing and planning learning activities, and evaluating learning processes and outcomes), affective strategies (e.g., reducing anxiety and fostering motivation), and social strategies (e.g., asking questions, collaborating with peers, and empathizing). Oxford utilizes this framework to develop the Strategy Inventory of Language Learning (SILL), a widely employed tool adapted for various second language learners to enhance their awareness of learning strategies.

O'Malley and Chamont (1990) introduce another recognized framework for understanding strategy usage, which categorizes strategies into metacognitive, cognitive, and socio-affective domains. Metacognitive strategies involve mental processes aimed at managing learning and performance by planning, monitoring, and assessing. Cognitive strategies encompass a range of specific learning techniques like repetition, categorization, note-taking, inference, transformation, and summarization. Socio-affective strategies involve interpersonal and emotional approaches, such as collaborating with others to gather feedback or share information.

Although definitions and parameters of learning strategies may vary, learning strategies discussed in second language studies commonly include four types: cognitive, metacognitive, social, and affective strategies. An unresolved issue revolves around whether these strategies should be incorporated into classroom instruction. While some researchers advocate for teaching strategies to enhance second language learning, others argue that classroom time should prioritize providing learners with opportunities for input and output. Despite the ongoing debate about the necessity of teaching strategies, based on their classroom teaching experiences, many educators and teachers point out that numerous language learners struggle to develop their own strategies independently and lack knowledge of effective strategies. To assist those interested in strategy instruction, several researchers have proposed guidelines for teaching strategies, a practice known as strategies-based instruction.

Strategies-Based Instruction

Strategies-based instruction (SSBI) refers to a type of learner-centered language education that integrates style and strategy training exercises into classroom language teaching (Cohen & Dörnyei, 2002; Oxford, 2001).

The essential idea behind this approach is to empower students not just with knowledge of what they can learn in language classes, but also with insights into how they can learn the language effectively.

The development of Strategies-Based Instruction has undergone a transformation over the years. In the 1960s, there was a shift towards focusing on the learner and on cultivating the ability to learn. Educators began to adopt insights from cognitive theory. In the 1970s, there emerged a more directive approach to language learner strategies, emphasizing what good language learners could teach us (Rubin, 1975). The 1980s witnessed attempts to categorize strategies. O'Malley and Chamot (1990), Oxford (1990), and others devised classification systems that categorized strategies based on whether they were primarily metacognitive, cognitive, social, affective, or other functions, drawing mainly from the extensive literature on first language reading strategies.

During the 1990s, there was a transition from simply describing and categorizing strategies to experimenting with various interventions in classroom settings. The focus shifted towards assessing whether learners could improve their language learning by either adopting new strategies or utilizing existing ones more efficiently. In the 2000s, there was a convergence towards structured strategies-based instruction. As strategy classification systems have been sorted out and categories become more fine-tuned, there is an increasing interest in understanding how specific tasks may align with particular learning style preferences and require specific language strategies. In other words, the one-size-fits-all approach is becoming custom fitted.

The strategies-based teaching approach now underscores the importance of incorporating both explicit and implicit methods in the language classroom. The primary goal of this approach is to support learners in enhancing their effectiveness in acquiring and utilizing the target language. Strategies-based instruction assists learners in fostering awareness about the variety of strategies they can utilize, understanding how to apply these strategies systematically and efficiently according to their individual learning styles, and learning when and how to transfer the strategies to unfamiliar language learning and usage situations. The basis of SSBI is built upon the following series of components (Cohen & Weaver, 2005):

1. Strategy Preparation
During this stage, the goal is to assess the extent of the learners' existing knowledge and ability in employing strategies. It is crucial not to presume that students possess no prior knowledge of strategy use. It is likely that they have already developed some strategies; however, the key consideration is whether they use these strategies systematically and effectively.

2. Strategy Awareness-Raising
In this phase, the aim is to introduce learners to strategies they may not have previously considered or may have thought about but never used. The SSBI tasks are purposely designed to increase students' overall awareness about: 1) the components of the learning process, 2) their

individual learning style preferences or general learning approaches, 3) the strategies they currently employ, as well as those suggested by the teacher or peers, 4) the amount of responsibility that they take for their learning, and 5) approaches that can be used to evaluate the students' strategy use for evaluating their strategy use. Awareness-raising activities inherently involve a direct and clear focus on strategies and their implementation.

3. Strategy Training

During this stage, students receive explicit instruction on how, when, and why specific strategies (whether used independently, in sequence, or in clusters) can aid in language learning and using tasks. In a typical classroom setting focused on strategy training, teachers illustrate, demonstrate, and provide examples of potentially beneficial strategies. They prompt students to share additional examples drawn from their own learning experiences, facilitate discussions in small groups or as a whole class about strategies (such as the rationale behind their use, planning approaches for particular activities, and evaluating the effectiveness of chosen strategies), and encourage students to explore a wide range of strategies.

4. Strategy Practice

During this stage, students are urged to explore and apply a diverse range of strategies. The assumption is not merely that understanding a strategy is sufficient. It is essential for learners to have ample opportunities to test these strategies across various tasks. These activities, designed to be conducive to strategy implementation, serve to reinforce previously introduced strategies and offer students a chance to practice them while engaging with the course content. These activities should include explicit references to the strategies being used in completion of the task. In other words, students either (a) plan the strategies for a specific task, (b) are directed to notice the use of particular strategies as they are being applied, or (c) reflect on their strategy use (and its effectiveness) after completing the activity.

5. Personalization of Strategies
During this phase, learners customize their understanding of the strategies they have acquired, assess their application of these strategies, and explore methods to transfer their use to different contexts.

In SSBI, it is the responsibility of curriculum writers and teachers to ensure that strategies are incorporated into daily class materials and are intertwined into language tasks, both explicitly and implicitly, to facilitate contextualized practice of these strategies.

As mentioned earlier, the initial step in SSBI involves assisting learners in understanding themselves better. Several approaches can aid learners in recognizing their personal styles, preferences, strengths, and weaknesses. A common method involves the use of a self-assessment questionnaire, where learners rate their agreement or disagreement with various statements on a scale. The Strategy Inventory for Language Learning (SILL) by Oxford (1990) has been widely used. Alternative methods for identifying styles and strategies, as well as bringing them to learners' awareness, include self-reports obtained through interviews, diaries, and think-aloud protocols (Macaro, 2001; O'Malley & Chamot, 1990). By employing these approaches, teachers can gain insight into students' inclinations. If carrying out the recommended SBI activity appears overwhelming, teachers can alternatively provide casual guidance inside and outside the classroom, focusing on beneficial strategies gathered from the self-assessment checklist or similar practices mentioned earlier. The following activity, adapted from Brown (2007), serves as an example of the kind of activity teachers can employ during class.

[SBI Activity Example]

Students first answer the self-checklist developed based on a maxim for good language learning as follows:

1. Lower inhibition
2. Encourage risk taking
3. Build self-confidence
4. Develop intrinsic motivation
5. Engage in cooperative learning
6. Use right-brain processes
7. Promote ambiguity tolerance
8. Practice intuition
9. Process error feedback

10. Set personal goals

Step 1. Learning style checklist

Select a single box in each item that most accurately reflects your characteristics. Boxes A and E suggest a strong resemblance to you. Boxes B and D imply a moderate resemblance. Box C indicates no preference.

	A	B	C	D	E	
1. I am not concerned about people laughing at me when I speak.						I feel embarrassed when people laugh at me while I speak.
2. I enjoy experimenting with new words and structures, even if I'm not entirely confident in them.						I prefer to use language that I know is correct.
3. I am highly confident in my ability to succeed in learning this language.						I feel uncertain about my chances of succeeding in learning this language
4. I want to learn this language because of what I can personally gain from it.						I am learning this language only because someone else is requiring it.
5. I really enjoy working with other people in groups.						I would much rather work alone than with other people.
6. I enjoy absorbing language and grasping the overall meaning of what is said or written.						I like to analyze the many details of language and understand exactly what is said and or written.

7. If there is a lot of language to learn, I simply focus on tackling one step at a time.						I feel very frustrated when confronted with a large amount of language material all at once.
8. I am not overly conscious of myself when I speak.						I 'monitor' myself very closely and consciously when I speak.
9. When I make mistake, I try to use them to learn something about the language.						When I make a mistake, it annoys me because that's symbol of how poor my performance is.
10. I actively search for ways to continue learning the language outside of the classroom.						I depend on the teacher and the activities in the classroom to provide me with everything necessary for success.

Step 2: Reflection

Afterward, students can participate in any or all of the following activities:

(1) discussing the reasons behind their responses in small groups,

(2) sharing their feelings in small groups regarding their responses,

(3) informally tallying the responses to each item,

(4) receiving informal advice from teachers based on their experiences about why certain practices may lead to success or failure, or

(5) arriving at the general agreement that responses falling

into categories A and B typically represent successful approaches to language learning.

Step 3: Introducing and using strategic techniques

Teachers present and/or employ strategic techniques aimed at enhancing students' areas of weakness. The table below provides a list of ways to build strategic techniques in a language classroom.

Areas	Activities
1. To lower inhibitions	Play guessing games and communication games; do role plays and skits; sing songs; use plenty of group work; have students share their fears in small group.
2. To encourage risk taking	The teacher praises students for making sincere efforts to try out language; use fluency exercise where errors are not corrected at that time; give outside-of-class assignments to speak or write.
3. To build students' self-confidence	The teacher tells students explicitly (verbally and nonverbally) that s/he does indeed believe in them; have students make lists of their strengths, of what they know or have accomplished so far in the course.
4. To help students develop intrinsic motivation	Remind students explicitly about the rewards for learning English; describe (or have students look up) jobs that require English.
5. To promote cooperative learning	Direct students to share their knowledge; play down competition among students; get students to think of themselves as a team; do a considerable amount of small-group work.
6. To encourage students to use right-brain processing	Use movies in class; have students read passages rapidly; do skimming exercises, do rapid 'free writes'; do oral fluency exercises where the object is to get students to talk a lot without being corrected,

7. To promote ambiguity tolerance	Keep theoretical explanations simple; deal with a few rules at a time; occasionally resort to translation into a native language to clarify a word or meaning
8. To help students use their intuition	Praise students for good guesses; do not always give explanations of errors; correct only selected errors
9. To get students to make their mistakes work for them	Record students' oral production and get them to identify errors; encourage students to make lists of their common errors and to work on them on their own
10. To get students to set their own goals	Explicitly encourage or direct students to go beyond the classroom goals; have them lists of what they will accomplish on their own in a particular week; get students to make specific time commitments at home to study the language

Dörnyei (2005) also suggests strategy instruction, which involves (a) enhancing learners' awareness and understanding of why strategies are used in second language learning, (b) introducing them to new strategies and demonstrating how to use them, (c) providing opportunities for learners to apply strategies, and (d) encouraging them to discuss the effectiveness of strategies. Below are some common methods used for teaching strategies to students:

1. Teacher modeling: Teachers show the cognitive, affective, and social process they use when approaching and carrying out a task by verbalizing these thoughts (i.e., think aloud).
2. Awareness raising: Teachers let students think about the strategies they used and how other strategies can help them to learn better. This can be done through teacher-led

discussion, small-group sharing, and learning diaries.

3. Guided practice: Teachers provide students with a set of guidelines and activities which then lead to planning which strategies to use, monitoring the use of strategies, and evaluating the effectiveness of the strategies.
4. Review, reflect, and reuse: Students are asked to review and evaluate the way they use strategies, and this enables them to distinguish useful ones from ineffective ones.

(Adapted from Goh, 2012, p. 73)

It is crucial to recognize that being aware of one's learning style and taking strategic actions extend beyond the classroom environment. Achieving mastery often involves learners' self-motivated endeavors to continue learning outside of formal classroom settings. Teachers play a pivotal role in assisting learners to progress towards autonomy by encouraging them to explore learning opportunities beyond the classroom.

Age

Things to Consider 8.8

1. Do you believe that the age at which learners start learning a second language influences their level of success? Can you explain why?
2. If you consider the timing of starting L2 learning significant, do you believe age outweighs other factors previously

discussed in determining the level of success?

It is widely believed that children generally outperform adults in acquiring a second language, a notion stemming from the Critical Period Hypothesis (CPH). The CPH suggests that animals, including humans, are naturally inclined to learn specific knowledge and skills during particular stages of life, initially proposed by Lenneberg (1967). Originally, the CPH aimed to explain first language acquisition, suggesting that learning language might be challenging or even impossible after puberty. While direct evidence supporting or refuting the CPH in first language acquisition is scarce due to children's early exposure to language, there are notable cases in the literature that shed light on the topic.

This was the case of Genie (Curtiss, 1977) and of several untamed children (discussed in Candland, 1993). Under such extremely detrimental circumstances, these adolescents could not learn their first language, and although a lot of efforts were made to teach them language after they were rescued, it was impossible for them to develop language to the level of their peers.

Further support for the Critical Period Hypothesis (CPH) in first language acquisition has emerged from studies focusing on delayed acquisition of first language among the deaf population (Mayberry & Lock, 2003; Newport, 1990). Unfortunately, around 90 percent of deaf children born to hearing parents do not encounter sign languages until they reach six years of age, thus postponing their acquisition of a first language until they begin formal education. Newport (1990) conducted a comparative analysis of deaf children: those exposed to American Sign Language (ASL) from birth (native signers), those who started learning ASL between four and six years old (early learners), and those who began ASL acquisition after the age of twelve (late learners). The research revealed that native signers exhibited more consistent usage of grammar markers compared to early learners, who in turn demonstrated more consistent usage than late learners. Similar findings were reported in subsequent research involving deaf children (Mayberry, 2007; Mayberry & Lock, 2003), offering further support for the CPH in first language acquisition.

CPH and Second Language Acquisition

The next logical inquiry revolves around whether the Critical Period Hypothesis (CPH) operates similarly in second language acquisition as it does in first language acquisition. Before discussing empirical research on the age effects concerning ultimate attainment in second language acquisition, it is crucial to introduce an alternative term used in Second Language Acquisition (SLA) literature – the sensitive period. Coined by Long (1990), this concept suggests a more gradual decline in language acquisition abilities, allowing for greater variation in attainment compared to the CPH. While the CPH predicts a rapid decrease in language learning ability, the Sensitive Period Hypothesis posits sensitivity to decline rather than absolute drop-offs, suggesting that the decline in learning may occur gradually over time.

Both anecdotal accounts and empirical research suggest that developing a native-like accent in a second language often requires early exposure, a view corroborated by various studies such as Ramsey and Wright (1974). However, there remains debate regarding whether adult learners can reach native-like proficiency in pronunciation. Neufeld (1979) proposed that enhanced teaching methods could improve learners' phonological abilities in specific tasks. While adults may be able to replicate native accents in short exercises, no teaching method has consistently demonstrated success in achieving native-like pronunciation in everyday communication. Nevertheless, the lack of conclusive evidence does not rule out the possibility of post-pubertal second language learners attaining pronunciation that is indistinguishable from that of native speakers. Several studies (Bongaerts, 1999; Ioup, Boustagui, El Tigi, & Moselle, 1994) have identified late second language learners who have achieved exceptional native-like proficiency in phonology.

What about other areas of the language? Numerous studies have explored the impact of age on second language morphosyntax, following pioneering work by Oyama (1976) and Patkowski (1980). These investigations aim to determine if age and morphosyntax proficiency are systematically linked. Researchers typically assess ultimate attainment by comparing second language learners' performance on grammaticality judgment tasks across different arrival ages, benchmarked against native speakers. For example, Johnson and Newport (1989) conducted a study involving 46 Chinese and Korean speakers learning English, all college-educated and residing in the US for at least five years. They completed a 276-item grammaticality judgment test. The findings revealed a significant negative correlation between age of arrival (ranging from 3 to 39) and grammaticality judgment scores. Particularly, this correlation was most pronounced in the 3 to 16 age group, but diminished in the 17 to 39 group. Young arrivals, aged 3 to 7, performed comparably to native speakers, while adolescents arriving between 8 and 16 showed declining performance with age. Adults arriving between 17 and 39 displayed erratic performance, with no clear relationship between age of arrival and grammaticality judgment scores. Unexpectedly, one learner who arrived at age 23 achieved an accuracy rate of 92%, on par with native speakers.

Birdsong and Molis (2001) conducted a replication of Johnson and Newport's (1989) study, but with a different group of individuals: 61 college-educated Spanish speakers who were learning English as a second language. Employing the same grammaticality judgment test used by Johnson and Newport, Birdsong and Molis found that those who arrived early (between ages 3 and 16) consistently achieved near-perfect scores without much variation. Conversely, a significant negative correlation was observed between those who arrived late and their test scores. Similar to Johnson and Newport's findings, there were also 13 individuals who arrived late (at 17 years or older) and achieved scores of 92 percent or higher.

The findings of Birdsong and Molis (2001) and Johnson and Newport (1989) may appear similar on the surface, particularly regarding the negative correlation between age of arrival and performance on the grammaticality judgment test, as well as the discovery of late arrivals who performed comparably to native speakers. However, a closer examination reveals differences between the two studies. Johnson and Newport (1989) specifically noted that only those who arrived very early (between 3 to 7 years old) attained native-like proficiency without any correlation between age and test scores. Conversely, the adolescent group (aged 8 to 16) displayed a significant negative correlation between age of arrival and test performance. In contrast, Birdsong and Molis (2001) found that learners arriving in the US up to the age of 16 not only achieved scores akin to native speakers but also showed no individual variations. Essentially, while Johnson and Newport identified the critical period as being around 7 years old, Birdsong and Molis suggested it extended to 16 years old. In essence, the critical period delineated in these studies was not consistent.

Bialystok (1997) questioned the notion of a critical period being the determining factor in second language acquisition success. Her examination focused on the acquisition of French gender marking by English and German speakers, revealing that the age at which learning commenced did not yield significant effects. Rather, the length of study or duration of stay in the target community appeared to be more influential in determining ultimate attainment. Additionally, through a reevaluation of Johnson and Newport's (1989) data, Bialystok and Hakuta (1994) discovered that not all linguistic structures were influenced by age. In other words, while some structures were indeed affected by the age of learning onset, others were not.

In summary, young children are more inclined to reach native-like proficiency in a second language, particularly in phonology, compared to adolescents or adults. However, there are notable instances of adult learners achieving native-like proficiency. Moreover, not all linguistic structures are equally influenced by the age at which second language learning begins. Consequently, the concept of a critical period in second language learning does not sufficiently explain age-related phenomena, as there appear to be multiple critical periods rather than one singular critical period. These critical periods can vary across different aspects of language, such as phonology, morphosyntax, syntax, and pragmatics, and may even differ within the same linguistic domain.

Explanations for Age-Related Phenomenon

When considering the role of age in second language learning, several explanations have been proposed. Some argue that neurological changes in adults hinder their ability to approach language-learning tasks in the same manner as children. As individuals age, there is a gradual lateralization of brain functions, resulting in a reduced availability of the neural resources required for language acquisition. Cognitive factors also play a role in explaining age-related differences in second language learning. The cognitive abilities possessed by adults may lead to less effective learning outcomes compared to children. Moreover, the distinct social contexts experienced by adults and children may influence language learning conditions. Generally, children benefit from more favorable conditions for language acquisition, including enhanced input and output opportunities through formal schooling. It is important to note that no single explanation can fully account for age-related disparities in language learning.

The question remains: "Is younger necessarily better?" Children generally benefit from more advantageous biological and social conditions for language learning. However, an early start does not guarantee success in second language acquisition (Burstall, 1975). It is not uncommon for early starters to feel discouraged and demotivated by slow progress. Moreover, if individuals who start early are not consistently exposed to second language input, they may be surpassed by those who begin later but receive ongoing exposure. Clearly, the age at which instruction begins is not the sole determinant of success in second language learning.

Chapter Summary

When reflecting on personal second language experiences or those of acquaintances, it is likely to observe how various individual characteristics discussed in this chapter relate to success or lack thereof in second language acquisition. However, attributing success solely to a specific element like motivation or personality is often challenging. This complexity arises from several factors. One key factor is that learner characteristics are interconnected; for example, when an English learner mentions frequent interactions with native speakers, this could be due to their outgoing nature, high motivation, or simply being surrounded by English speakers. Moreover, individuals may respond differently to diverse situations; they might perceive themselves as introverted in unfamiliar settings but extroverted among friends. Additionally, assessing learner characteristics and success in second language acquisition poses difficulties. Defining 'successful learning' varies among researchers, leading to different measurement tools being employed. For instance, success could be defined as grammatical accuracy, necessitating a grammar test, or as communicative abilities, requiring an oral examination. Consequently, research into individual differences in second language learning demands meticulous interpretation. Nevertheless, studies underscore the importance for educators to consider learners' individual differences and create environments conducive to second language learning success.

References

Abdullah, M., & Jacobs, G. (2004). Promoting cooperative learning at primary school. *TESL-EJ, 7*(4), n4.

Abraham, R. G. (1981). *The relationship of cognitive style to the use of grammatical rules by Spanish-speaking ESL students in editing written English.* Unpublished doctoral dissertation. University of Illinois at Urbana-Champaign.

Abraham, L. B. (2008). Computer-mediated glosses in second language reading comprehension and vocabulary learning: A meta-analysis. *Computer Assisted Language Learning, 21*(3), 199-226.

Adams, R. (2007). Do second language learners benefit from interacting with each other? In A. Mackey (Ed.) *Conversational interaction in second language acquisition* (pp. 30-51). Oxford University.

Alderson, J. C., & Hudson, R. (2013). The metalinguistic knowledge of undergraduate students of English language or linguistics. *Language Awareness, 22*(4), 320-337.

Alghamdi, R., & Gillies, R. (2013). The impact of cooperative learning in comparison to traditional learning (small groups) on EFL learners' outcomes when learning English as a foreign language. *Asian Social*

Science, 9(13), 19.

Baralt, M., & Gurzynski-Weiss, L. (2011). Comparing learners' state anxiety during task-based interaction in computer-mediated and face-to-face communication. *Language Teaching Research*, 15(2), 201-229.

Basturkmen, H., Loewen, S., & Ellis, R. (2002). Metalanguage in focus on form in the communicative classroom. Language Awareness, 11(1), 1-13.

Bialystok, E. (1982). On the relationship between knowing and using linguistic forms1. *Applied Linguistics, 3*(3), 181-206.

Bialystok, E. (1997). The structure of age: In search of barriers to second language acquisition. *Second Language Research, 13*, 116-137.

Bialystok, E., & Hakuta, K. (1994). *In other words: The science and psychology of second language acquisition*. New York: Basic Books.

Bialystock, E., & Sharwood Smith, M. (1985). Interlanguage is not a state of mind: An evaluation of the construct for second language acquisition. *Applied Linguistics, 6*, 101-117.

Bitchener, J. (2004). The relationship between the negotiation of meaning and language learning: A longitudinal study. *Language Awareness, 13*(2), 81-95.

Birdsong, D. (1999). Introduction: Whys and why nots of the critical period hypothesis for second language acquisition. In D. Birdsong (Ed.), *Second language acquisition and the critical period hypothesis* (pp. 1-22). Mahwah, NJ: Lawrence Erlbaum Associates.

Birdsong, D., & Molis, M. (2001). On the evidence for maturational constraints in second-language acquisition. *Journal of Memory and Language, 44*, 235-249.

Blake, R. (2000). Computer mediated communication: A window on L2 Spanish interlanguage. *Language Learning & Technology, 4*, 120-136.

Blake, R. J. (2011). Current trends in online language learning. *Annual Review of Applied Linguistics, 31*, 19-35.

Bongaerts, T. (1999). Ultimate attainment in L2 pronunciation: The case of very

advanced late L2
learners. In D. Birdsong (Ed.), *Second language acquisition and the critical period hypothesis* (pp. 133-159). Mahwah, NJ: Lawrence Erlbaum Associates.

Brown, H. D. (2007). *Teaching by principles: An interactive approach to language pedagogy*. NY: Pearson Longman.

Brown, H. D. (2014). *Principles of language learning and teaching: A course in second language acquisition*. Pearson.

Brown, R. (1973). *A first language: The early stages*. Cambridge, MA: Harvard University Press.

Brumfit, C. (1984). *Communicative methodology in language teaching: The roles of fluency and accuracy*. Cambridge: Cambridge University Press

Bueno-Alastuey, M. C. (2013). Interactional feedback in synchronous voice-based computer mediated communication: Effect of dyad. *System, 41*(3), 543-559.

Burstall, C. (1975). *Collaborative action research for English language teachers*. Cambridge: Cambridge University.

Burt, M. K. (1975). Error analysis in the adult EFL classroom. *TESOL Quarterly, 9*, 53-63.

Canale, M., & Swain, M. (1980). Theoretical bases of communicative approaches to second language teaching and testing. *Applied Linguistics, 1*, 1-47.

Candland, D.H. (1993). *Feral children and clever animals*. New York: Oxford University Press.

Carroll, J. (1981). Twenty-five years in foreign language aptitude. In K. Diller (Ed.), *Individual differences and universals in language learning aptitude* (pp. 83-118). Rowley, MA: Newbury House.

Celce-Murcia, M. (2014). An overview of language teaching methods and approaches. In M. Celce-Murcia, D. Brinton, & M. A. Snow (Eds.), *Teaching English as a second or foreign language* (4th ed.)(pp. 2-14). Boston: National Geographic Learning.

Chapelle, C., & Roberts, C. (1986). Ambiguity tolerance and field independence as predictors of proficiency in English as a second language. *Language Learning, 36*, 27-45.

Chaudron, C. (1988). *Second language classrooms*. Cambridge: Cambridge University Press.

Chomsky, N. (1959). Review of B. F. Skinner. Verbal Behavior, *Language, 35*, 26-58.

Chomsky, N. (1965). *Aspects of the theory of syntax*. Boston, MA: MIT Press.

Clarke, M., & Silberstein, S. (1977). Toward a realization of psycholinguistic principles in the ESL reading class. L*anguage Learning, 27*, 135-154.

Cohen, A. D., & Dörnyei, Z. (2002). Focus on the language learner: Motivation, styles, and strategies. *An Introduction to Applied Linguistics, 14*, 170-190.

Cohen, A. D., & Weaver, S. J. (2005). *Styles and strategies-based instruction: A teachers' guide*. Center for Advanced Research on Language Acquisition, University of Minnesota.

Cook, V. (1997). *Inside language*. London: Edward Arnold.

Cook, V. (2003). *Effects of the second language on the first*. Clevedon, UK: Multilingual Matters.

Corder, S. P. (1967). The significance of learners' errors. *International Rearview of Applied Linguistics, 5*, 161-170.

Corder, S. P. (1969). *An intermediate English practice book*. Madras: Orient Longmans.

Curran, C. (1972). *Counseling-learning: A whole person model for education*. NY: Grune & Stratton.

Curtiss, S. (1977). *Genie: A psycholinguistic study of a modern- day "wild child"*. New York: Academic Press.

Danesi, M. (1988). Neurological bimodality and theories of language teaching. *Studies in Second Language Acquisition, 10*(1), 13-31.

Deci, E. (1975). *Intrinsic motivation*. New York: Plenum Press.

Dekeyser, R. (1998). Beyond focus on form: Cognitive perspectives on learning and practicing second language grammar. In C. Doughty & J. Williams

(Eds.), *Focus on form in classroom language acquisition* (pp. 42-63). New York: Cambridge University Press.

DeKeyser, R. (2000). The robustness of critical period effects in second language acquisition. *Studies in Second Language Acquisition, 22*, 493-533.

DeKeyser, R. (2001). Automaticity and automatization. In P. Robinson (Ed.), *Cognition and second language instruction* (pp. 125-151). Cambridge: Cambridge University Press.

DeKeyser, R. M. (2007a). Conclusion: The future of practice. In R. DeKeyser (Ed.), *Practice in a second language: Perspectives from applied linguistics and cognitive psychology* (pp. 287-304). Cambridge University Press.

DeKeyser, R. (Ed.). (2007b). Practice in a second language: *Perspectives from applied linguistics and cognitive psychology*. Cambridge University Press.

DeKeyser, R. (2020). Skill acquisition theory. In B. VanPatten & J. Williams (Eds.), *Theories in second language acquisition* (pp. 97-113). Routledge.

Dörnyei, Z. (1995). On the teachability of communication strategies. *TESOL quarterly, 29*(1), 55-85.

Dörnyei, Z. (1997). Psychological processes in cooperative language learning: Group dynamics and motivation. *The Modern Language Journal, 81*(4), 482-493.

Dörnyei, Z. (2001a). *Motivational strategies in the language classroom*. Cambridge: Cambridge University Press.

Dörnyei, Z. (2001b). *Teaching and researching motivation*. Harlow: Longman.

Dörnyei, Z. (2005). *The psychology of the language learner: Individual differences in second language acquisition*. Mahwah, NJ: Lawrence Erlbaum Associates.

Dörnyei, Z., & Csizér, K. (1998). Ten commandments for motivating language learners: Results of an empirical study. *Language Teaching Research, 2*, 203-229.

Dörnyei, Z., & Ottó, I. (1998). Motivation in action: A process model of L2 motivation. *Working Papers in Applied Linguistics, 4*, 43-69.

Dörnyei, Z., & Skehan, P. (2003). Individual differences in second language learning. In C. Doughty & M. Long (Eds.), *The handbook of second language acquisition* (pp. 589-630). Blackwell Publishing.

Donato, R. (1994). Collective scaffolding in second language learning. In J. P. Lantolf and G. Appel (Eds.), *Vygotskian approaches to second language research* (pp. 33–56). Norwood, NJ: Ablex.

Doron, S. (1973). *Reflectivity-impulsivity and their influence on reading for inference for adult students of ESL*. Unpublished manuscript, University of Michigan.

Doughty, C. (1991). Second language instruction does make a difference: Evidence from an empirical study of SL relativization. *Studies in Second Language Acquisition, 13*, 431-469.

Doughty, C., & Pica, T. (1986). "Information gap" tasks: Do they facilitate second language acquisition? *TESOL Quarterly, 20*, 305-325.

Doughty, C. J. (2003). Instructed SLA: Constraints, compensation, and enhancement. In C. Doughty & M. Long (Eds.), *The handbook of second language acquisition* (pp. 256-310). Blackwell Publishing.

Doughty, C., & Williams, J. (1998). *Focus on form in classroom second language acquisition*. Cambridge University Press.

Duffy, G. (1993). Rethinking strategy instruction: Four teachers' development and their low achievers' understandings. *The Elementary School Journal, 93*(3), 231-247.

Dušková, L. (1984). Similarity – an aid or hindrance in foreign language learning? *Folia Linguistics, 18*, 103-115.

Edge, J., & Garton, S. (2009). *From experience to knowledge in ELT*. Oxford: Oxford University Press.

Ehrman, M. E. (1996). *Understanding second language learning difficulties*. Thousand Oaks, CA: Sage Publications.

Ellis, N. (1993). Rules and instances in foreign language learning: Interactions of explicit and implicit knowledge. *European Journal of Cognitive*

Psychology, 5(3), 289-318.

Ellis, N. (2007). The weak interface, consciousness, and form-focused instruction: Mind the doors. In H. Nassaji & S. Fotos (Eds.), *Form-focused instruction and teacher education* (pp. 17-34). Oxford University Press.

Ellis, R. (1990). *Instructed second language acquisition*. Cambridge: Basil Blackwell.

Ellis, R. (2001). Introduction: Investigating form-focused instruction. *Language Learning, 51*, 1-46.

Ellis, R. (2003). *Task-based language learning and teaching*. Oxford University Press.

Ellis, R. (2005). Measuring implicit and explicit knowledge of a second language: A psychometric study. *Studies in Second Language Acquisition, 27*(2), 141-172.

Ellis, R. (2008). The study of second language acquisition (2nd ed). Oxford University Press.

Ellis, R. (2009). Implicit and explicit learning, knowledge and instruction. In R. Ellis, S. Loewen, C. Elder, J. Philp, & H. Rinders (Eds.), *Implicit and explicit knowledge in second language learning, testing and teaching* (pp. 3-25). Multilingual Matters.

Ellis, R. (2012). *Language teaching research and language pedagogy*. Hoboken: Wiley-Blackwell.

Ellis, R., Basturkmen, H., & Loewen, S. (2001). *Learner uptake in communicative ESL*. Language Learning, 51, 282-318.

Ellis, R., Loewen, S., & Erlam, R. (2006). Implicit and explicit corrective feedback and the acquisition of L2 grammar. *Studies in Second Language Acquisition, 28*, 339-368.

Ewing, T. E. (1980). Paleogene tectonic evolution of the Pacific Northwest. *The Journal of Geology, 88*(6), 619-638.

Færch, C., Haastrup, K., & Phillipson, R. (1984). *Learner language and language learning*. Clevedon, UK: Multilingual Matters.

Ferris, D. (2010). Second language writing research and written corrective feedback in SLA: Intersections and practical applications. *Studies in Second Language Acquisition, 32*, 181-201.

Fries, C. C. (1945). *Teaching and learning English as a foreign language*. Ann Arbor, Michigan: University of Michigan Press

García Mayo, M. P. (2002). Interaction in advanced EFL pedagogy: A comparison of form-focused activities. *Interactional Journal of Educational Research, 37*, 323-341.

Gardner, R. C. (1985). *Social psychology and second language learning: The role of attitudes and motivation*. London: Edward Arnold.

Gass, S. (2003). Input and interaction. In C. Doughty & M. H. Long (Eds.), *The handbook of second language acquisition* (pp. 224-255). Oxford: Basil Blackwell.

Gass, S., & Mackey, A. (2006). Input, interaction and output: An overview. In K. Bardovi-Harlig & Z. Dörnyei (Eds.), *AILA Review* (pp. 3-17). Amsterdam: John Benjamins.

Gass, S., & Selinker, L. (2008). *Second language acquisition: An introductory course*. NY: Routledge.

Gass, S., Svetics, I., & Lemelin, S. (2003). Differential effects of attention. *Language Learning, 53*, 497-545.

Gass, S., & Varonis, E. (1989). Incorporated repairs in NNS discourse. In M. Eisentein (Ed.), *Variation and second language acquisition* (pp. 71-86). New York: Plenum.

Gass, S., & Varonis, E. (1994). Input, interaction and second language production. *Studies in second language acquisition, 16*, 283-302.

Gatbonton, E., & Segalowitz, N. (2005). Rethinking communicative language teaching: A focus on access to fluency. *Canadian Modern Language Review, 61*(3), 325-353.

Goh, C. (2012). *Learner strategies*. The Cambridge guide to pedagogy and practice in second language teaching. Cambridge University Press.

Goldschneider, J. M., & DeKeyser, R. (2001). Explaining the natural order of L2 morpheme acquisition in English: A meta-analysis of multiple determinants. *Language Learning, 51*, 1-50.

Goodman, K. (1967). Reading: A psycholinguistic guessing game. *Journal of the Reading Specialist, 6*, 126-135.

Gregg, K. (1984). Krashen's monitor and Occam's razor. *Applied Linguistics, 5*, 79-100.

Han, Z-H. (2004). *Fossilization in adult second language acquisition*. Clevedon, UK: Multilingual Matters.

Han, Z. (2008). On the role of meaning in focus on form. In Z Han (Ed.), *Understanding second language process* (pp. 45-79). Multilingual Matters.

Han, Z., Park, E. S., & Combs, C. (2008). Textual enhancement of input: Issues and possibilities. *Applied Linguistics, 29*(4), 597-618.

Hoffman, M. L. (1986). Affect, cognition and motivation. In R. M. Sorrention & E. T. Higgins (Eds.), *Handbook of motivation and cognition* (pp. 244-280). NY: Guilford.

Hoffman, S. Q. (1997). Field dependence/independence in second language acquisition and implications for educators and instructional designers. *Foreign Language Annals, 30*, 222-234.

Horwitz, E. K., Horwitz, M. B., & Cope, J. (1986). Foreign language classroom anxiety. *Modern Language Journal, 70*, 125-132.

Hulstijn, J. H., & De Graaff, R. (1994). Under what conditions does explicit knowledge of a second language facilitate the acquisition of implicit knowledge? A research proposal. *AILA Review, 11*(97-112).

Hymes, D. (1971). *On communicative competence*. Philadelphia: University of Pennsylvania Press.

Ioup, G., Boustagui, E., El Tigi, M., & Moselle, M. (1994). Reexamining the critical period hypothesis: A case study of successful adult SLA in a naturalistic environment. *Studies in Second Language Acquisition, 16*, 73-

98.

Ishihara, N., & Cohen, A. D. (2010). *Teaching and learning pragmatics: Where language and culture meet*. Harlow, England: Longman Pearson Education.

Jamieson, J. (1992). The cognitive styles of reflection/impulsivity and field independence/dependence and ESL success. *The Modern Language Journal, 76*(4), 491-501.

Johnson, D. W., & Johnson, R. T. (1994). *Leading the cooperative school*. International Book Co.

Johnson, D. W., Johnson, R. T., & Holubec, E. (1998). *Cooperation in the classroom*. Boston.

Johnson, J., & Newport, E. (1989). Critical period effects in second language learning: The influence of maturational state on the acquisition of ESL. *Cognitive Psychology, 21*, 60-99.

Johnson, J., & Newport, E. (1991). Critical period effects on universal properties of language: The status of subjacency in the acquisition of a second language. *Cognition, 39*, 215-258.

Kagan, J. (1965). Reflection-impulsivity and reading ability in primary grade children. *Child Development, 36*, 609-628.

Kagan, S., & Kagan, S. (1994). *Cooperative learning*. San Clemente: Kagan.

Kagan, S. (1989). The structural approach to cooperative learning. Educational leadership, 47(4), 12-15.

Keefe, J. W. (1979). Learning style: An overview. In J. W. Keefe (Ed.), *Student learning styles: Diagnosing and prescribing programs* (pp. 1-17). Reston, VA: National Association of Secondary School Principals.

Kellerman, E. (1987). *Aspects of transferability in second language acquisition*. Unpublished doctorial dissertation, Katholieke Universiteit te.

Kim, J. H. (2011). Learner interpretation of teacher corrective intention of feedback in EFL classrooms. E*nglish Language & Literature Teaching, 17*(1), 81-99.

Kim, J. H. (2016). The effects of different types of oral corrective feedback on the development of explicit/implicit L2 knowledge of English articles. *English Teaching, 71*(3), 53-77.

Kim, J. H., & Han, Z-H. (2007). Recasts in communicative EFL classes: Do teacher intent and learner interpretation overlap? In A. Mackey (Ed.), *Conversational interaction in second language acquisition: A collection of empirical studies* (pp. 269-297). Oxford: Oxford Press.

Kim, Y., & McDonough, K. (2008). The effect of interlocutor proficiency on the collaborative dialogue between Korean as a second language learners. *Language Teaching Research, 12*(2), 211-234.

Krashen, S. (1982). *Principles and practices in second language acquisition.* London: Pergamon.

Krashen, S. (1983). The relationship between theory and practice. In R. Blair (Ed.) *Innovative approaches to language teaching and language learning* (pp. 15-30). New York: Newbury House.

Krashen, S. (1984). *Writing: Research, theory and application*. Oxford: Pergamon Institute of English.

Krashen, S. (1985). *The input hypothesis: Issues and implications*. New York: Longman.

Krashen, S. (2004). *The power of reading: Insights from the research*. Portsmouth, NH: Heinemann.

Krashen, S., & Terrell, T. (1983). *Natural approach*. New York: Pergamon.

Lantolf, J. P. (2000). *Sociocultural theory and second language learning*. Oxford: Oxford University Press.

Lantolf, J. P. (2005). Sociocultural and second language learning research: An exegesis. In E. Hinkel (Ed.), *Handbook of research in second language teaching and learning* (pp. 335-354). NY: Routledge.

Larsen-Freeman, D. (1997). Chaos/Complexity Science and Second Language Acquisition. *Applied Linguistics, 18*, 141-165.

Larsen-Freeman, D., & Anderson, M. (2011). *Techniques and principles in language teaching*. Oxford: Oxford University Press.

Lee, J., & VanPatten, B. (2003). *Making communicative language teaching happen*. Boston: McGraw-Hill.

Leeser, M. J. (2004). Learner proficiency and focus on form during collaborative dialogue. *Language Teaching Research, 8*(1), 55-81.

Lenneberg, E. (1967). *Biological foundations of language*. New York: John Wiley.

Leow, R. (1997). Attention, awareness, and foreign language behavior. *Language Learning, 47*, 467-505.

Li, S. (2010). The Effectiveness of Corrective Feedback in SLA: A Meta-Analysis. *Language Learning, 60*, 309-365.

Li, S. (2013). The interactions between the effects of implicit and explicit feedback and individual differences in language analytic ability and working memory. *Modern Language Journal, 97*, 634-654.

Lightbown, P. (1983). Exploring relationships between developmental and instructional sequences in L2 acquisition. In H. Seliger & M. H. Long (Eds.), *Classroom oriented research in second language acquisition* (pp. 217-243). Rowley, MA: Newbury House.

Lightbown, P. (1985). Great expectations: Second language acquisition research and classroom teaching. *Applied Linguistics, 6*, 173-189.

Lightbown, P. M., & Spada, N. (1990). Focus on form and corrective feedback in communicative language teaching: Effects on second language learning. *Studies in Second Language Acquisition, 12*, 429-448.

Lightbown, P. M., & Spada, N. (2006). *How languages are learned*. Oxford: Oxford University Press.

Littrell, S., Fugelsang, J., & Risko, E. F. (2020). Not so fast: Individual differences in impulsiveness are only a modest predictor of cognitive reflection. *Personality and Individual Differences, 154*, 109678.

Loewen, S. (2004). Uptake in incidental focus on form in meaning-focused ESL lessons. *Language Learning, 54*(1), 153-188.

Loewen, S. (2011). Focus on form. In E. Hinkel (Ed.), *Handbook of research in second language teaching and learning* (pp. 576-592). Routledge.

Loewen, S. (2015). *Introduction to instructed second language acquisition*. NY: Routledge.

Loewen, C., Erlam, R, & Ellis, R. (2009). The incidental acquisition of third person -s as implicit and explicit knowledge. In R. Ellis, S. Loewen, C. Elder, J. Philp, & H. Rinders (Eds.), *Implicit and explicit knowledge in second language learning, testing and teaching* (pp. 262-280). Multilingual Matters.

Loewen, S., & Nabei, T. (2007). Measuring the effects of oral corrective feedback on L2 knowledge. In A. Mackey (Ed.), *Conversational interaction in second language acquisition: A collection of empirical studies* (pp. 361-377). Oxford: Oxford Press.

Long, M. (1983). Linguistics and conversational adjustments to non-native speakers. *Studies in Second Language Acquisition, 5*, 177-193.

Long, M. H. (1990). Maturational constraints on language development. *Studies in Second Language Acquisition, 12*, 251-285.

Long, M. H. (1991). Focus on form: A design feature in language teaching methodology. In K. de Bot, R. Ginsberg, & C. Kramsch (Eds.), *Foreign language research in cross-cultural perspective* (pp. 39-52). Amsterdam: John Benjamins.

Long, M. H. (1996). The role of the linguistic environment in second language acquisition. In W. Ritchie & T. Bhatia (Eds.), *Handbooks of second language acquisition* (pp. 413-468). San Diego, CA: Academic Press.

Long, M. (2003). Stabilization and fossilization in interlanguage development. In C. Doughty & M. H. Long (Eds.), T*he handbook of second language acquisition* (pp. 487-535). Malden, MA: Blackwell.

Long, M. H. (2007). *Problems in SLA*. Mahwah, NJ: Lawrence Erlbaum Associates.

Long, M. H., & Robinson, P. (1998). Focus on form: Theory, research, and practice. In C. Doughty & J. Williams (Eds.), *Focus on form in classroom second language acquisition* (pp. 16-42). Lawrence Erlbaum.

Loschky, L. (1994). Comprehensible input and second language acquisition: What is the relationship? *Studies in Second Language Acquisition, 16*, 303-323.

Lynch, T. (1997). Nudge, nudge: teacher interventions in task-based learner talk. *ELT Journal, 51*, 317-325.

Lyster, R. (1998). Recasts, repetitions, and ambiguity in L2 classroom discourse. *Studies in Second Language Acquisition, 20*, 51-81.

Lyster, R., & Ranta, L. (1997). Corrective feedback and learner uptake: Negotiation of form in communicative classrooms. *Studies in Second Language Acquisition, 19*, 37-66.

Lyster, R., & Saito, K. (2010). Oral feedback in classroom SLA: A meta-analysis. *Studies in Second Language Acquisition, 32*, 265-302

Mackey, A. (1999). Input, interaction, and second language development: An empirical study of question formation in ESL. *Studies in Second Language Acquisition, 21*(4), 557-587.

Mackey, A. (2006). Feedback, noticing and instructed second language learning. *Applied Linguistics, 27*(3), 405-430.

Mackey, A. (2012). *Input, interaction and corrective feedback in L2 classrooms.* Oxford: Oxford University Press.

Mackey, A., Gass, S., & McDonough, K. (2000). Learners' perceptions about feedback. Studies in Second Language Acquisition, 22, 471-497.

Mackey, A., & Goo, J. (2007). Interaction research in SLA: A meta-analysis and research synthesis. In A. Mackey (Ed.), *Conversational interaction in second language acquisition: A series of empirical studies* (pp. 407-452). Oxford: Oxford University Press.

Mahinpo, B. (2012). Kagan cooperative learning model: The bridge to foreign language learning in the third millennium. *Theory and Practice in Language Studies, 2*(6), 1134-1140.

Macaro, E. (2001). Analyzing student teachers' codeswitching in foreign language classrooms: Theories and decision making. *The modern language journal, 85*(4), 531-548.

Masgoret, A. M., & Gardner, R. C. (2003). Attitudes, motivation, and second language learning: A meta–analysis of studies conducted by Gardner and associates. *Language Learning, 53*, 123-163.

Mayberry, R. I. (2007). When timing is everything: Age of first-language acquisition effects on second-language learning. *Applied Psycholinguistics, 28*, 537-549

Mayberry, R. I., & Lock, E. (2003). Age constraints on first versus second language acquisition: Evidence for linguistic plasticity and epigenesis. *Brain and Language, 87*, 369-384,

McCafferty, S. G. (Ed.). (2006). *Cooperative learning and second language teaching*. Cambridge University Press.

McGroarty, M. (1989). The benefits of cooperative learning arrangements in second language instruction. *NABE journal, 13*(2), 127-143.

McLaughlin, B. (1987). *Theories of second language learning*. London: Edward Arnold.

McLaughlin, B. (1990). *Restructuring. Applied Linguistics, 11*, 113-128.

Messick, S. (1984). The nature of cognitive styles: Problems and promise in educational practice. *Educational Psychologist, 19*(2), 59-74.

Nassaji, H., & Fotos, S. (2004). Current developments in research on the teaching of grammar. *Annual Review of Applied Linguistics, 24*, 126-145.

Nassaji, H., & Fotos, S. (2011). *Teaching grammar in second language classrooms: Integrating form-focused instruction in communicative context*. NY: Routledge.

Nassaji, H. (2020). Assessing the effectiveness of interactional feedback for L2 acquisition: Issues and challenges. *Language Teaching, 53*(1), 3-28.

Neufeld, G. (1979). Towards a theory of language learning ability. *Language Learning, 29*, 227-241.

Newman, F., & Holtzman, L. (1993). *Lev Vygotsky: Revolutionary scientist*. New

York, NY: Routledge.

Newport, E. (1990). Maturational constraints on language learning. *Cognitive Science, 14*, 11-28.

Nicholas, H., Lightbown, P. M., & Spada, N. (2001). Recasts as feedback to language learners. *Language Learning, 51*, 719-758.

Nunan, D. (1999). *Second language teaching and learning.* Boston, MA: Heinle Cengage Learning.

Nunan, D. (2005). *Task-based language teaching*. Cambridge: Cambridge University Press.

O'Dowd, R. (2011). Online foreign language interaction: Moving from the periphery to the core of foreign language education? *Language Teaching, 44*(3), 368-380.

Ohta, A. S. (2001). *Second language acquisition processes in the classroom: Learning Japanese*. Routledge.

O'Malley, J. M., & Chamont, A. (1990). *Learning strategies in second language acquisition*. Cambridge: Cambridge University Press.

Olsen, R. E. W-B., & Kagan, S. (1992). About cooperative learning. In C. Kessler (Ed.), *Cooperative language learning: A teacher's resource book* (pp. 1–30). Englewood Cliffs, NJ: Prentice Hall.

Oxford, R. L. (1990). Language learning strat

Ortega, L. (2009). *Understanding second language acquisition*. NY: Routledge

Oxford, R. (1990). *Language learning strategies: What every teacher should know*. New York: Newburry House.

Oxford, R. (1993). *Style analysis survey (SAS)*. University of Alabama.

Oxford, R. (1999). Learning strategies. In B. Spolsky (Ed.), *Concise encyclopedia of educational linguistics* (pp. 518-522). Oxford: Elseviet.

Oxford, R. (2011). Strategies for learning a second or foreign language. *Language Teaching, 44*, 167-180.

Oyama, S. (1976). A sensitive period for the acquisition of a nonnative phonological system. *Journal of Psycholinguistic Research, 5*, 261-283.

Pasfield-Neofitou, S. (2012). *Online communication in a second language: Social interaction, language use, and learning Japanese*. Multilingual Matters.

Patkowski, M. (1980). The sensitive period for the acquisition of syntax in a second language. *Language Learning, 30*, 449-472.

Pavlov, I. P. (1932). *The reply of a physiologist to psychologists.*

Pica, T. (1994). Research on negotiation: What does it reveal about second-language learning conditions, processes, and outcomes? *Language Learning, 44*(3), 493-527.

Pica, T., Kanagy, R., & Falodun, J. (1993). Choosing and using communicative tasks for second language instruction. In G. Crookes & S. M. Gass (Eds.), *Tasks and language learning* (pp. 9-34). Multilingual matters.

Ramsey, C. A., & Wright, E. N. (1974). Age and second language learning. *The Journal of Social Psychology, 94*, 115-121.

Rebuschat, P. (2013). Measuring implicit and explicit knowledge in second language research. *Language Learning, 63*(3), 595-626.

Reid, J. M. (1987). The learning style preferences of ESL students. *TESOL Quarterly*, 21, 87-111.

Reid, J., & Powers, J. (1993). Extending the benefits of small-group collaboration to the ESL writer. *TESOL Journal, 2*(4), 25-32.

Reinking, J. A., Hart, A. W., & von der Osten, R. (2002). *Strategies for successful writing*. Englewood Cliff, NJ: Prentice Hall.

Renandya (Eds.), *Methodology in language teaching: An anthology of current practice* (pp. 295–302). Cambridge: Cambridge University Press.

Richards, J. C. (1998). *Beyond training: Perspective on language teacher education*. Cambridge: Cambridge University Press.

Richards, J., & Renandya, W. (2002). *Methodology in language teaching: An anthology of current practice*. Cambridge: Cambridge University Press.

Richards, J. C., & Rodgers, T. S. (2014). *Approaches and methods in language teaching.* Cambridge University Press.

Robinson, P. (2001). Individual differences, cognitive abilities, aptitude complexes and learning conditions in second language acquisition. *Second Language Research, 17*, 368-392.

Robinson, P. (2005). Cognitive complexity and task sequencing: Studies in a componential framework for second language task design. *IRAL-International Review of Applied Linguistics in Language Teaching, 43*(1), 1-32.

Rollinson, P. (2005). Using peer feedback in the ESL writing class. *ELT Journal, 59*, 23-30.

Romiszowski, A., & Mason, R. (2013). Computer-mediated communication. In T. Savelyeva, M. Spector, D. Merrill, J. Elen, MJ. Bishop. (Eds), *Handbook of research on educational communications and technology* (pp. 402-436). Routledge.

Rubin, J., Thompson, I., & Sun, H. (1982). *How to be a more successful language learner*. Boston: Heinle & Heinle.

Sato, M., & Ballinger, S. (2012). Raising language awareness in peer corrective feedback: A cross-context, cross-methodology examination. *Language Awareness, 21*, 151-179.

Schachter, J. (1974). An error in error analysis. *Language Learning, 24*, 205-214.

Schmidt, R. (1990). The role of consciousness in second language learning. *Applied Linguistics, 11*, 129-158.

Schmidt, R. (1995). Consciousness and foreign language learning: A tutorial role on the role of attention and awareness in learning. In R. Schmidt (Ed.), *Attention and awareness in foreign language learning* (pp. 1-64). Honolulu: University of Hawai'i at Manoa, Second Language Teaching and Curriculum Center.

Schmidt, R. (2001). Attention. In P. Robinson (Ed.), *Cognition and second language instruction* (pp. 3-32). Cambridge: Cambridge University Press.

Schmidt, R., & Frota, S. (1986). Developing basic conversational ability in a second language: A case study of an adult learner of Portuguese. In R. Day (Ed.), *Talking to learn: Conversation in second language acquisition* (pp. 237-326). Rowley, MA: Newbury House.

Schwartz, B. (1993). On explicit and negative data effecting and affecting competence and linguistic behavior. *Studies in Second Language Acquisition, 15*, 147-163.

Segalowitz, N. (2003). Automaticity and second languages. In C. Doughty & M. H. Long (Eds.), *The handbook of second language acquisition* (pp. 382-408). Malden, MA: Blackwell.

Selinker, L. (1972). Interlanguage. *International Review of Applied Linguistics, 10*, 209-231.

Shaaban, K., & Ghaith, G. (2005). The theoretical relevance and efficacy of using cooperative learning in the ESL/EFL classroom. *TESL Reporter, 38*(2), 14-28.

Sharwood Smith, M. (1986). Comprehension versus acquisition: two ways of processing input. *Applied Linguistics, 7*, 239-256.

Sharwood Smith, M. (1991). Speaking to many minds: On the relevance of different types of language information for the L2 learner. *Second Language Research, 7*, 118-132.

Sharwood Smith, M. (1993). Input enhancement in instructed SLA: Theoretical bases. *Studies in Second Language Acquisition, 15*, 165-179.

Sharwood Smith, M., & Kellerman, E. (1989). The interpretation of second language output. In H. W. Dechert & M. Raupach (Eds.), *Transfer in language production* (pp. 217-235). Norwood: Ablex.

Skehan, P. (1989). *Individual differences in second language learning*. London: Edward Arnold.

Skehan, P. (1991). Individual differences in second language learning. *Studies in Second Language Acquisition, 13*(2), 275-298.

Skehan, P. (1996). A framework for implementation of task-based instruction. *Applied Linguistics, 17*, 38-62.

Skehan, P. (1998). *A cognitive approach to language learning*. Oxford: Oxford University Press.

Skinner, B. F. (1965). *Science and human behavior*. Simon and Schuster.

Smith, B. (2009). The relationship between scrolling, negotiation, and self-initiated self-repair in an SCMC environment. *CALICO journal, 26*(2), 231-245.

Stevick, E. W. (1982). *Teaching and learning languages* (Vol. 32). Cambridge: Cambridge University Press.

Sparks, R., Dale, P., & M. Patton, J. (2023). Individual differences in L1 attainment and language aptitude predict L2 achievement in instructed language learners. *The Modern Language Journal, 107*(2), 479-508.

Storch, N. (2002). Patterns of interaction in ESL pair work. *Language Learning, 52*(1), 119-158.

Storch, N. (2005). Collaborative writing: Product, process, and students' reflections. *Journal of Second Language Writing, 14*, 153–173.

Swain, M. (1983). Bilingualism without tears. *On TESOL, 82*, 35-46.

Swain, M. (1985). Communicative competence: Some roles of comprehensible input and comprehensible output in its development. In S. Gass & C. Madden (Eds.), *Input in second language acquisition* (pp. 235-253). Rowley, MA: Newburry House.

Swain, M. (1996). Integrating language and content in immersion classrooms: Research perspectives. *Canadian Modern Language Review, 4*, 529-548.

Swain, M. (2000). The output hypothesis and beyond: Mediating acquisition through collaborative dialogue. *Sociocultural Theory and Second Language Learning, 97*(1), 97-114.

Swain, M., & Lapkin, S. (1998). Interaction and second language learning: Two adolescent French immersion students working together. *Modern Language Learning, 82*, 320-337.

Swain, M., & Lapkin, S. (2002). Talking it through: Two French immersion learners' response to reformulation. *International Journal of Educational Research, 37*(3), 285-304.

Torrance, E. (1980). *Your style of learning and thinking*. Athens: University of

Georgia Press.

Truscott, J. (1996). The case against grammar correction in L2 writing classes. *Language Learning, 46*, 327-369

VanPatten, B. (1993). Grammar teaching for the acquisition of rich classroom. *Foreign Language Annals, 26*, 435-450.

VanPatten, B. (1996). *Input processing and grammar instruction in second language acquisition*. Norwood, NJ: Ablex.

Vygotsky, L. S. (1978). *Mind in society: The development of higher psychological process*. Cambridge, MA: Harvard University Press.

Vygotsky, L. S. (1986). *Thought and language-revised edition*. Boston: MIT.

Vygotsky, L. S. (1987). Thinking and speech. In R. W. Rieber & A. S. Carton (Eds.), *The Collected Works of L.S. Vygotsky. Volume 1: Problems of General Psychology* (pp. 37-285). New York: Plenum Press.

Watanabe, Y., & Swain, M. (2007). Effects of proficiency differences and patterns of pair interaction on second language learning: Collaborative dialogue between adult ESL learners. *Language Teaching Research, 11*(2), 121-142.

Wesche, M. (1981). Language aptitude measures in streaming, matching students with methods, and diagnosis of learning problems. In K. C. Diller (Ed.), *Individual differences and universals in language learning aptitude* (pp. 119-139). Rowley, MA: Newbury House.

White, L. (1989). *Universal grammar and second language acquisition.* Amsterdam: John Benjamins.

White, L. (1991). Adverb placement in second language acquisition: some effects of positive and negative evidence in the classroom. *Second Language Research, 7*, 133-161.

Wigglesworth, G., & Storch, N. (2009). Pair versus individual writing: Effects on fluency, complexity and accuracy. *Language Testing, 26*(3), 445-466.

Wilkins, D.A. (1976). *Notional Syllabuses*. Oxford: Oxford University Pres

Winitz, H. (1981). *The comprehension approach to foreign language instruction.*

Rowley, MA: Newbury House Publishers.

Wong, W. (2005). *Input enhancement: From theory and research to the classroom*. Higher Education.

Yamaoka, T. (2005). From item learning to category learning: A learning process of procedural knowledge of learning. *ARELE, 16*, 21-30.

Zobl, H. (1980). The formal and developmental selectivity of L1 influence on L2 acquisition. *Language Learning, 30*, 43-57.

About the Author

Ji Hyun Kim

Ji Hyun Kim is a professor in the Department of English Education at Keimyung University. She completed her bachelor's degree at Ewha Womans University and obtained a master's degree from the State University of New York. She earned her doctoral degree in Applied Linguistics/TESOL from Teachers College at Columbia University in New York. Her extensive publications focus on instructed second language acquisition, covering topics such as corrective feedback, learner perception, second language writing, and the cognitive processes involved in second language learning.